Simply Grace

Torn Curtain Publishing
Wellington, New Zealand
www.torncurtainpublishing.com

© Copyright 2023 Janet O'Halloran-Westerman. All rights reserved.

ISBN Softcover 978-0-473-67018-4
ISBN EPub 978-0-473-67019-1

No portion of this book may be reproduced, stored in a retrieval system or transmitted in any form or by any means—electronic, mechanical, photocopy, recording or otherwise—except for brief quotations in printed reviews or promotion, without prior written permission from the author.

All details included in this book are written from the author's best recollection and perspective. Names of people included in this book are used with permission. Some names and places have been changed to preserve anonymity. This book is not intended as a substitute for professional counselling or advice.

Scripture quotations are taken from the Holy Bible, New King James Version®. Copyright © 1982 by Thomas Nelson. Used by permission. All rights reserved.

Cover photograph used with permission of author.

Cataloguing in Publishing Data
  Title: Simply Grace
  Author: Janet O'Halloran-Westerman
  Subjects: Christian living, faith and spirituality, self-help, inspirational, personal memoir

Typeset in Deutschlander, Helvetica, Poppins and Minion Pro

A copy of this title is held at the National Library of New Zealand.

Simply Grace

STORIES OF HUMOUR, FAITH
AND PERSEVERANCE

Janet O'Halloran-Westerman

Author's Note

This book is a selection of treasured moments and memories that have been woven together to form the tapestry of my life. I have also recounted times and seasons I would rather not think about, yet they need to be told. Most of all, I have written to honour those who have touched my life in special ways and who probably never understood how profound and impacting their influence has been on me.

I am blessed to have special people around me who have been kind enough to listen as I have recounted experiences from my past. At the encouragement of these friends, I am sharing some of my life with you. This is a collection of short stories that are not necessarily chronological but rather are snapshots of God's grace through the ups and downs of life. As such, they can be read in any order. I give you permission to laugh with me and cry with me, and hopefully my journey will cause you to reflect on your own story and those who have impacted your life in special ways.

You will get to meet my precious family, my husband Geoff, and my children Cameron, Kimberley, and son-in-law Aaron. Within these pages you will also meet my wider family and people from my present and past. You will read, in my story, about a woman who was deeply broken and had no hope, a woman who, despite turning her back on her faith at times, came to understand that a loving God never turned His back on her. There are miracles, and moments where the seemingly impossible becomes possible.

Happiness is not something that can be bought. It's not birthed out of a fantastic life full of mountaintop experiences. Often happiness comes through painful experiences and simply making it through hardships that felt like battlegrounds in our lives. True happiness, not the social media photoshopped kind, is something that can be seen by the twinkle in an elderly person's eyes when they get to sit with their family, or the feeling you get by admiring the sunset at the end of a long hard day.

I guess a lot of my life has been like that—happiness borne out of nothing more than having made it through each of life's valleys.

I hope my words bring encouragement to you. Most of all I hope this book helps you recognise the moments of happiness in your life, a life that is full of ups and downs, cracks and potholes, but in reality, is also a treasure chest of moments and experiences that make you the invaluable person you are today.

Contents

Author's Note

REMEMBERING	*1*
THE BLOSSOM TREE	*13*
ONE MOMENT IN TIME	*21*
OMA'S SONG	*28*
THE WHISTLE MAN	*39*
THE DRAGON	*45*
AN INHERITANCE	*60*
WHEELS WITH WINGS	*68*
LOVE CONQUERS ALL	*73*
TRUE WORTH	*81*
TILL WE MEET AGAIN	*85*
BE YOURSELF	*93*
SIMON	*97*
A MIRACLE	*102*
THE BIBLE TELLS ME SO	*108*
TE MONA	*114*
FRIENDSHIP	*118*

A Glimpse   123

These Boots Are Made For Walking   128

Things Are Going To Change   134

A Blessing   143

Lifting My Burden   152

Heartbeat   155

Found   164

Cliff Diving   175

Anchored   187

Acknowledgements   204

- 1 -

Remembering

Clunk, clunk, clunk, bang! My eyes dart to the left and then to the right. *Clunk, clunk, clunk, bang. Clunk, clunk, clunk, bang!* I am six years old, sitting in my beautiful, crisp, homemade dress, in the second row from the front at church. It's coming up to midday, and the sun is starting to appear through the high windows. The brightness is causing me to squint in an effort to hit my target.

Looking down, I admire my black patent-leather shoes and white lace-edged ankle socks. *How could shoes of such beauty, bordering on magical in my mind, also make such gratifying noises?* I kick the legs of my chair from side to side, and then, quick as a wink, the seat of the chair in front of me. Three clunks from side to side, then a swift kick forward, and *bang!*

It requires perfect aim and concentration to miss the buttocks of the hapless person sitting on the seat in front of me, but with my mischievousness now honed to perfection, I always seem to get away with it. Well, almost.

On less successful Sundays, my dad would bring shame to my growing reputation as a church clown and come marching down the aisle, scoop me up, and in the most undignified manner, cart me out to the car.

This embarrassing performance of extracting me from my seat was not something that could be managed in secret or go unnoticed. My father fully embodied the Dutch genetic trait of being the tallest race of people in the world. In my mind, his oversized feet were no less noisy than Bigfoot stomping through a forest disturbing everyone and everything in its path.

On one level I felt it was a win-win situation. Instead of sitting through yet another sermon, I would manage to disturb the whole church and then get to sit in the sunshine and enjoy the warmth of the family car.

Sermon time generally involved me making missiles out of paper or honing my magic trick skills by rolling up a handkerchief in my hand then hiding it somewhere on my person and pulling it out dramatically like a magician would a dove or a rose.

Every week my sisters and I would have already sat through an hour-long Sunday School class and then another hour of church, so by this time the fidgeting would reach new heights of kicking, giggling, and pinching one another along the row.

The car, even though hot and sticky with its plastic protective covers still tightly covering the seating, was not such a bad place to be on a nice sunny day.

Dad's discipline, although not pleasant, was far more agreeable to me than the dreaded weekly encounter with the terrifying church bully. A sweet cherub of a girl, she was always in the prettiest of frocks and usually wore a bow in her hair. She was a product of being the only girl in a family of older brothers, who it appeared kept her well-schooled in the art of stealth and attack.

Being forcibly removed spared me running the gauntlet to get past the bully each week after church. Running the gauntlet would generally fail, as she would hide in the shadows and wait for me to come flying past. Just as I thought I had slipped past the enemy, she would pounce. She had the appearance of an angel, but her menacing grimace amounted to what my six-year-old mind perceived to be a devil coming at me.

It was always the same trick. The bully would lift a large family Bible above her head and proceed to slam me on the head with it as hard as she could.

Whack!

She would howl with laughter as I ran to the car terrified that she would come after me. The words 'Bible-bashing' were a literal experience for me almost on a weekly basis.

The attacks continued for a number of years. Even when I grew tall and she remained shorter, the bullying continued. Her mental hold over me was by this time complete, and although she now had great difficulty reaching up to swing the Bible over my full height, I was so programmed into submission that I was almost bowing down to receive my expected weekly whack on the head.

The astounding thing was this little girl was smaller than me and I could have overpowered her in an instant, but for some reason that thought never entered my mind. Like many problems in life, I allowed myself to believe she was a giant with her arms outstretched over my head. But she never was a giant. I had only allowed her to become that powerful in my childish mind.

It's a funny thing, but when you are a child you never imagine that other people live completely different lives to you. My life as one of three girls born to Dutch immigrants included close friendships with other Dutch families and the families within our local church.

Mum and Dad worked hard to become what they perceived to be upstanding New Zealand citizens and to embrace all aspects of New Zealand life. On some level it was as if they felt they were lesser people for being immigrants and worked tirelessly to be seen as the perfect New Zealand family. This was an impossible task which took a lot of physical and mental energy. Even so, New Zealand was seen as a safe refuge and an opportunity for a fresh start after coming from war-torn Holland.

For some reason my parents went against the prevailing thinking of the time in one area in particular. It was the notion that children should be taught to speak only one language, an idea that thankfully has been refuted today. Sadly, this meant that many lost the ability to understand and speak their ancestral tongue, but in our case my parents spoke English in public and a mix of Dutch and English at home. Often the sentences used would be a mix of languages, and as a result even today I sometimes have to stop and think whether or not the word I am about to use is Dutch rather than English.

My parents had us well versed in the language of public Dutch admonition with a verbal clip around the ears. Many times they smiled sweetly in public while muttering in Dutch some wild punishment that was supposedly going to take place when we got home. There were also times when a hilarious quick-witted comment from either of my parents in Dutch would have us all in suppressed hysterics, the reason for which only our family would understand.

Being the child of immigrants gave me a perspective that enables me to understand people who come from other cultures and are trying to make New Zealand their home.

As a child, I never knew that some people didn't attend church, or that there were churches that looked different from my own. My parents attended the Salvation Army church which was well known for its outreach to the destitute and homeless and its fight against social injustices. The Salvation Army was founded in London's East End in 1865. It was born out of the vision of a young man called William Booth during a dark time when poverty blanketed parts of London and people were living in appalling conditions. William Booth and his wife, Catherine, recognised that in addition to spiritual rebirth, people needed physical, emotional and social restoration.

William and Catherine, along with their supporters, eventually came up with a quasi-military command structure, which allowed for quick decisions and fast implementation of church policy. The uniform they wore as part of their movement gave them instant recognition wherever they went in London, and eventually the world, with their message of Christianity and social reformation.

Underlying everything was the hope of helping people understand their great value in the sight of God, and letting them know that they were loved in spite of their background and history, and that every man, woman and child is of great value to God.

Being surrounded by uniforms and military terminology at church each Sunday was my norm. As a little girl, I didn't know that others may have seen us as different and maybe even peculiar. Later in life, I realised that we really weren't that different—it was a Christian message, but with a military twist.

A lot of Salvation Army churches are noisy, vibrant places of worship. Our church had a brass band, and we all learned to play the tambourines. People would call out in support of what was being preached with the words 'amen' and 'hallelujah' often resounding across the building during the service. Sometimes in the evening service, a local drunk would venture in and sit at the back and often yell abuse at the 'officer' who was preaching, which didn't seem to faze him or her at all.

Now here's the problem I had with church. As a six-year-old, I couldn't formulate this problem in words or even put thoughts around it, as it was emotional and I didn't grasp emotions and what they meant, I just had them. Each Sunday morning at about the same time, it would peer around the corner at me. Then it would well up slowly, like a pain unattached to any part of me yet was everywhere within me. It lived somewhere deep inside, deeper than my physical being. I couldn't fidget it away, and I couldn't toss it in the creek that wound its way around the back of the church, in the hope it would swim off like a fish and never come back.

It always came back.

I was a master of disguise and hid the problem with snickering, talking, fidgeting, chair kicking, and whatever other nonsense came into my head.

The general congregational entertainment was another great distraction, and I enjoyed that to its fullest. One elderly man (in reality, he was probably only fifty at a push) had hearing aids that would randomly make loud beeping sounds which few had the courage to inform him about. The noise was much like a small siren and would distract us from whatever was going on at the front. His wife was the master of dirty looks, and if any of us made the smallest of sounds, she would twist her entire body towards us and give us her infamous death stare. We found this quite amusing considering her husband's hearing aids made more noise than all of our noises put together.

Then there was the lady who often sat in a row not far behind me who loved to sing but freely admitted she was completely tone deaf. She sang loud, very loud. Even as a child I admired her bravery. That voice, like a cat with its head trapped in a tin can, was another source of great entertainment to me.

There was always something going on to amuse and entertain us.

Prayer time in most churches today is no less heartfelt but certainly less physical than when I was a child. Many of the adults chose to pour out their petitions to God on their knees, resting their arms on the seats of their chairs. Clasping their hands together, they would close their eyes and humbly kneel to pray. Not everyone chose to pray this way, but it was quite acceptable if you did.

The presiding officer when I was a young girl was a lady with physical dimensions that were curvy to say the least. Each week as she turned around to kneel and pray, we children would wait with bated breath as her black skirt would rise and expose to the entire congregation white bloomers that went down to her knees! She exposed no skin at all, but in my eyes, it was a moment worth waiting for and was the height of hilarity to a row full of children.

Although we found lots to laugh about, we knew on a deeper level we were loved by these church members we called Salvationists, and though not often said out loud, that love was like an invisible embrace around our young, impressionable hearts.

⁓

To my discomfort and annoyance each week, even with all the distractions going on around me, 'it' came back. This thing that had no name always returned at around the same time, generally midday when my stomach decided it was time to head home and eat. The twisting of a hungry tummy was like a double whammy with the twisting of my emotional pain.

Every week after the sermon, an invitation was given to anyone who wanted to come forward and open their life up to God's love. I generally hadn't listened to much of what was said during the sermon, so why when this call was given did this immensely uncomfortable and strange emotion always come rolling over me?

I was only six years old at the time and had no understanding that I was being gently touched by the Holy Spirit who was calling this little girl's heart to receive His love and His presence in my life. I didn't grasp that our creator doesn't force Himself upon anyone, but gives us the choice to respond to Him.

It wasn't about the four walls of the church. God's Spirit can't be boxed up into a building, but is everywhere and can touch us anywhere at any time. Even so, it was in church that I first felt the touch of God. It was as if the heartfelt call that resounded at the end of the sermon each week was just for me.

The next two years passed in a whirl of activity. There was Girls' Brigade on Tuesdays, and gymnastics on Thursdays followed by fish and chips. Every week we had swimming lessons at the Boys' and Girls' Institute, and of course there was school to attend during the week and often barbecues and picnics with our Dutch adopted families on the weekends.

We lived next door to a family who also attended the Salvation Army and had four children. Many hours were spent with this family who loved us like their own. We climbed trees, built forts, and took turns running up and down the street pushing each other in an old cane pram. We had water guns we would squirt at passing cars, and an overgrown section nearby that was like an adventure playground for children. Life was hectic, mostly fun, and full to say the least.

Our family also had the wonderful experience of travelling by ship on the *MS Angelina Lauro* back to the Netherlands. There we spent six months living with our Opa (granddad) and extended family before travelling another six weeks by ship back home again. This trip sounds idyllic, and in many ways it was. But I spent much of the journey in the ship's infirmary with a gripping stomach-ache and nausea. I remember lying in a hospital bed hearing my dad arguing loudly with the ship's doctor who wanted to take my appendix out. My dad, never one to shy away from a good argument, was yelling, "No quack is going to cut open my daughter on this ship!" Thankfully, Dad was right and I didn't require surgery, but I can still remember the nausea and pain that overwhelmed me for weeks.

In hindsight, I believe I had what is called 'abdominal migraine' because I continued to have similar bouts of sickness throughout my childhood that were never fully explained.

At our church back in New Zealand, there was a group called Junior Soldiers which we could join from the age of eight. There we were taught about God, the Bible and the Salvation Army. It had a reputation for being lots of fun and full of rowdy activities. After I joined, I found it certainly lived up to that reputation. We sang songs about 'marching in the light of God', accompanied by stomping of feet and the swinging of our arms backwards and forwards as high as we could. We acted out all our songs with great enthusiasm. This often involved climbing on our chairs, or riding invisible horses or chariots, as we engaged in great heroics for God in our minds. I'm not sure that we fully understood all the concepts we sang about, but as far as fun was concerned, we took it to the maximum and had a great time.

In my childish enthusiasm, I sometimes took the fun side of Junior Soldiers beyond its limits. I would run with the other children out through the door of the Sunday School, through the room where all the band instruments were kept, and into the empty church hall where we would proceed to run around the seating, yelling our own version of the songs we had been singing. On occasion, our leader would run after us calling out dire warnings of what was to become of us when we grew up. I even remember him shouting as he ran after us once that we were so badly behaved, we would eventually all land up in the nearby young offender's prison that sat behind high wire and electric fences on the hill as you drove into our home town. His predictions ran off us like water off a duck's back as we continued our rousing rabble around the church hall.

Looking back as an adult, I still feel slightly mortified at the trouble we caused this leader. He was just an earnest young man who gave up his time each week to teach us spiritual matters, but when he gave us free range with our action songs, we took it too far. We were never told what we had to believe. At the end of the day, it was about making our own choices as we learned about God and life and listened to stories from the Bible in a way that a group of eight to thirteen year olds could understand.

This brings me to my second church-related problem: the only prerequisite to joining Junior Soldiers was that we had to be a Christian. Even as an eight-year-old child I knew in my heart I wasn't a Christian.

How I knew this, I do not know. I simply understood that God doesn't look at appearances or what church you attend; it doesn't even matter if you have never graced the doors of a church. I knew that God looks at the heart of a person and that is what matters to Him. God wanted a relationship with me, and at this time I didn't have that. I was like a mime artist acting out something that wasn't real inside of me.

So, in spite of outward appearances, I knew this one truth, and it was that in the secret place of my heart I had not yet opened my life up to God and I was not a Christian.

I continued to squirm in my seat each Sunday at the call to open my heart to God. My behaviour was still rambunctious, to say the least. No one would have guessed that behind the disagreeable behaviour was the inner turmoil of a child who was hiding behind an invisible door from the love of God. Not a soul knew of my dilemma regarding joining this group called Junior Soldiers. I doubt very much that many took it so seriously. Why I did, I can't tell, particularly as I viewed most of life as a big joke, but it consumed my thinking for weeks.

Then, a light bulb moment came. It was so simple and yet so obvious. How had I not seen it before? I would simply write a letter to God, ask Him if I was a Christian, and wait for His written reply. I reasoned that Sunday afternoon would be the best time; it was after all God's special day. So, I waited excitedly for Sunday to come.

The big day arrived. My plan was to be activated! The morning was filled with the usual Sunday rush. Mum was busy peeling potatoes and other vegetables in preparation for the Sunday roast. We girls all had our chores to do before getting dressed in our good clothes and then flying out the door to Sunday School which started an hour before the church service. On sunny days we would walk to Sunday School, and when it wasn't sunny, Dad would drop us off and return later with Mum for the church service.

It was a different world, one where little girls in their pretty homemade dresses would walk the one and a half kilometres without adult supervision to church. We never felt unsafe, even when a man once stopped to give us lollies.

Occasionally a mentally challenged boy who lived halfway along our route would run out of his house and chase us with a golf club. We found this rather hilarious and would run away laughing. I never felt he was upset; it was just a sort of game he played to get a reaction, and oh what reaction he got! Screaming and giggling girls, the twinge of fear I felt as he waved his golf club while chasing me—it was part thrilling and part terrifying. He only ever kept up his chase for a short time. Then he would turn and head back home and peace would be restored.

That afternoon, when church was over and lunch finished, I began to put my plan into action. I found a piece of cardboard from a box. I ripped it to approximately the size of an A4 piece of paper and in large lettering (I figured that if my writing was too small it might not be noticed by God) I wrote in my tidiest handwriting:

> Dear God,
>
> I don't know if I am a Christian.
>
> If I am, please sign here:
>
> ....

I left my note on the little play table made by Dad in the bedroom

I shared with my sister Caroline. I then skipped off to the lounge to play with my sisters. Every Sunday afternoon, Dad would play his favourite record on the stereo. He listened to all sorts of music—Burl Ives, the Sound of Music, or quite often a record of The Salvation Army Band. Dad would soon doze off, and Mum would sit in her armchair knitting.

I thought that being outside was more fun than listening to my parents' choice of music. I'd rather go and sit on top of the letterbox at the end of our driveway and wave at traffic (which I often did) than listen to the *paarp, paarp, boom!* of yet another Salvation Army band.

That Sunday afternoon dragged on. I made numerous trips to my bedroom, but every time I checked the letter, there was no reply from God.

I have a lasting memory of my parents that has stayed with me throughout my life. If I ever got up around their bedtime to use the toilet or get a drink of water, I would see the same thing. I saw it hundreds of times during my childhood as I walked past their bedroom. My mum would be on one side of the bed and my dad on the other—they would be on their knees, elbows resting on their bed, faces buried in their hands as they quietly talked to God.

Sometimes it's as if God moves out of the spiritual dimension and enters our physical world as other people become His hands and feet. I think of this as being touched by 'Jesus with skin on' as a person enables Jesus to work through them.

That Sunday afternoon, 'Jesus with skin on' came to me in the form of my dad who walked into my room and discovered my letter. Dad took me to my parents' bedroom and knelt beside the bed. I knelt down with him. Together we talked to God and asked Him to walk with me through life. We prayed that He would watch over me and that I would know His love all my life.

There were no thunderclaps, no tears, just silence. But when I stood up, I knew something had changed. I had opened my heart up to God, and inside me was a peace I had previously not had. Even as a child I recognised the change, and from that moment forward, the unwanted emotion I called "it" didn't trouble me anymore. I can't say my behaviour improved dramatically, and my pursuit of fun was still a large part of my nature, but there was a new strength within me. I knew there was a God, and that He loved me and watched over me.

∼

We can all look back at times in our lives and see situations that defy natural explanation. That day with my dad, as I opened my heart to God, it wasn't as if it was an introduction—He had always been with me—but that was the moment we began a relationship. Instead of God being a distant presence and something that I'd always accepted existed, He became my friend.

The years would pass, and that friendship would ebb and flow and sometimes would be stretched to the limit, but it would remain. Within these stories you will see my human frailties laid out before you, some good, some bad. I hope you enjoy the read and see something within these pages that either helps you on some level or just plain brightens up your day.

- 2 -

The Blossom Tree

The grass was damp beneath us as we sat at the far end of the school field. We tucked our dresses under our bottoms to protect us from the wet grass and hurriedly ate our lunches. Lunch consisted of Marmite and lettuce sandwiches wrapped in greaseproof paper and an apple to finish it off. Thirst was always quenched at the drinking fountain on the way back to class.

Today was an important day. My best friend Chrissy had promised to tell me the answer to the all-important question: *Where do babies come from?* I reasoned that if anyone might know the answer to the mystery regarding babies it would be Chrissy. After all, she had a lot of brothers and sisters and more just kept arriving.

Throughout my childhood I had two special friends—Lynda, who lived next door, and Chrissy. Both impacted my life in different yet special ways. This must have been a defining moment in my relationship with Chrissy because all these years later I can still remember how it was a cloudless day, how brightly the sun shone, and even the spot where we sat on the damp grass.

Chrissy and I were eleven years old and had been close friends since the day we met as five-year-olds starting school. She was like an explosion of giggling loveliness in my young world. She had copper red hair, and freckles splashed all over her face like thousands of small stars lighting up a galaxy. We looked so different, me with blonde hair and not a freckle in sight.

That wasn't the only difference between us. Chrissy came from a home of thirteen children, and they went to the Catholic church. I had two sisters, and we attended the Salvation Army church. Both churches were positioned on the main road of our hometown, right next door to each other.

I loved staying at Chrissy's house. There were bunk beds lining the bedrooms and children everywhere. Big pots of food would be bubbling away on the stove. Chrissy's mum would be perspiring in the heat of all the rising steam. Wiping her hands on her apron, she would then push her hair off her freckled face.

At dinner, highchairs were lined up. At some point one of the highchair occupants would pick up his or her plate and stick it upside down on top of their heads, then laugh uproariously while the food dribbled down their face. It was bedlam, and I loved it. Alternatively, I think Chrissy came to our house to stay just to get a good night's sleep!

On this particular day, sitting on the school field, I was holding my breath. Chrissy had finally finished her lunch and was about to tell me her version of 'the facts of life'. She knew where babies came from, and for the first time in my life, I was about to hear all about it.

A photograph records a moment in time; a picture is frozen in that place forever. That's how that moment sitting on the grass is to me. I heard what she said, let it sink in, and then I felt the blood rush to my face. I was shocked. I felt embarrassed that she would even talk about ladies' and men's private parts and then weave it into this fantastical story. We were best friends, yet she thought she could tell me a pack of lies and get away with it! What she told me was so disgusting and the weirdest thing I ever heard. I felt deceived, and to make matters worse she kept on saying, "But it's the truth!" I decided that either she was the worst friend in the world, or there was a grain of truth in what she said and I would need time to think about it.

Funny thing was, if I had only asked my mother, I am sure she would have told me. But for some reason I thought Chrissy would be the fountain of all knowledge in this department. Clearly babies kept arriving at her house and I figured she might have seen one or two flying in the window or appearing miraculously in the cot. I decided to forgive Chrissy, but I was disappointed that she felt she had to make up this stupid story.

Chrissy and I would dream dreams and talk about what we were going to be when we grew up. I was going to be a teacher and she was either going to be a nurse or work with animals. I was at a crossroads with my decision because if teaching wasn't for me I was going to be a famous roller-skater. I would amaze everyone I knew with my talent, which I would keep hidden until I made it onto the world stage. Then everyone would see how majestic my roller-skating flips and moves were, especially the school bullies who would soon regret ever being mean to me.

Imagination is a wonderful thing in a child. It has no limits and helps us escape from the mundane and also painful things in life and gives us hope for a brighter future.

Chrissy's family moved out of town not long after our facts of life discussion. As I grew older, from time to time I would think about Chrissy and the dreams we had. Had hers come to pass? One day I would find out. Meanwhile my life was to take a very different road to the blissful imaginations I'd had as a child.

It's probably a good thing we don't know the journey in front of us. Had I known the road ahead, I'm sure I wouldn't have coped with the prospect of what was about to come. I was going to walk into a valley that would sometimes be so dark I would be unable to see the way in front of me.

After finishing school, with no idea of what I wanted to do with my future, I took on jobs which were many and varied, one of which was tripping around in a double-decker bus for a radio station called 2ZB. I had a wonderful time wearing a bee costume and posing as the now mostly forgotten character called Buzz O'Bumble as we travelled to different locations entertaining children. Eventually, I decided to study nursing. By the time I was twenty-two I had graduated and took my first job as a practice nurse in a medical centre.

In the year before my graduation, I got invited to a party by another nurse in my class. As nurses we knew how to work hard and we knew how to have fun, so off to the party I went. On arrival I soon realised why we had been invited. There were few females, and clearly, "invite your nurse friends" had been an effort to bring gender balance to an otherwise male-dominated affair. I decided to take my exit not long after arrival.

I was almost at the door when a good-looking guy in a blue sweatshirt, flared jeans and jandals started a conversation with me. He introduced himself, and his name was Geoff. I hadn't noticed him in the crowd, so I stayed for a short chat. Within half an hour I knew I had met my husband. How I knew, I had no idea, but I did. I told my mother that evening I had met my husband. She found this rather humorous as I had not long finished a relationship and she no doubt thought my revelation about meeting my husband was going to blow over in a week.

We married, and looking back I now understand how right he was for me. Within three years I gave birth to our son, Cameron, and then two years later, our daughter, Kimberley. Our family was complete. Life was to be lived, and I was looking forward to the years ahead with my beautiful family. Little did I know that life was about to change. Ahead of me was a journey I had not planned.

I lay in bed, hardly daring to breathe in case it made the pain I was feeling in my head any worse. I held my head in my hands motionless, as if my hands were some sort of poultice that would remove the invisible swelling and drain the pain away. My knees scrunched up to my belly in an effort to relieve the all-encompassing nausea that rolled over me. Sounds became like distant echoes, and when I opened my eyes, spots and lights flashed before me.

The first time it happened, it was like some sort of craziness came raging through my front door uninvited. My women's cycle had returned after the birth of our second baby, and this time it had a new face, an ugly one that lived only in nightmares. I'd had menstrual cramps before I had children, but never had I experienced the blinding force of a hormonal migraine, nor did I know that this was to become a regular feature in my life. If it had lasted for a day I might have managed better, but sometimes these beasts would visit for up to eight days.

With a baby and a toddler to care for, I didn't have time for this. Medications were a failure. They caused my blood pressure to soar, and other pain relief was useless. My husband would find me on the bathroom floor with my head hanging in the toilet bowl or in bed with a bucket wrapped around my face. The only hope was when a doctor was called to our home and I was given an injection to knock me out until the migraine had hopefully passed.

Failing that, Geoff would call for an ambulance as I could no longer walk to the toilet. Dehydration had weakened me to the point where I couldn't lift my head up and I would be lying in my own vomit. The paramedics would have to roll me onto the stretcher as I had no physical power left.

To confuse matters, I had developed a second type of headache when I was nursing. Around the age of nineteen, I began having sinus infections. It was as if the sinus pain was trying to enslave me. I remember the first time I got a sinus headache and from there I just kept loading up on over-the-counter pain relief. These headaches would eventually become like a weight on my face. When I leaned forward, pus-like mucus would run from my nose. My teeth hurt, my face hurt, my nose was permanently blocked and when I lay down, I felt as if I was suffocating. My immune system seemed to be an enemy rather than a friend, and I got sick with any small infection that came along.

I had not long given birth to my son when I had my first of six sinus surgeries, all of which were equally unpleasant. The surgeries were often followed by infections during recovery time. Sinus headaches were a daily part of my life for twenty years.

The *pièce de résistance* was a headache that developed not long after my daughter was born. Often waking me up, this unfriendly night-time visitor felt like a claw on the back of my head, pulsing and throbbing to the point that it felt like the back of my skull was being crushed.

This mysterious headache dogged me for years. If only I'd owned what is a common accessory in many household first aid kits today—a blood pressure monitor—I could have had the beginnings of an answer. For some unknown reason I had developed a disease called malignant hypertension. This manifests as extremely uncontrollable and dangerously high blood pressure and is often resistant to treatment. Over the years that followed, I spent countless hours sitting in hypertension clinics and in the emergency department of our local hospital. At one point, I was accompanying my father into hospital for a heart attack and ended up being admitted myself after my blood pressure was taken when I didn't feel well.

After years of battling malignant hypertension, I was admitted to Mercy Hospital in Auckland for a relatively new procedure known as a renal denervation. On admission to the hospital, it was discovered I had developed severe renal stenosis (narrowing of a renal artery) secondary to the malignant hypertension, and for this I would require a renal stent. At a cost of thirty thousand dollars, I hoped these procedures would bring miraculous healing.

The procedures alone were not miraculous, but the medications I was previously resistant to now began to do their job and my blood pressure began to lower and was much improved. My final hormonal migraine thankfully welcomed the beginning of a reasonably early menopause, and although menopause generally has a bad rap, for me it heralded the start of a new life.

There's a place I know well, a place where some people live. I call it *The Shadowland*. It's where others like myself, living with situations that no matter how hard they try they cannot escape from, learn to live. They live two lives.

Residents of the Shadowland recognise that in their neediness and desperation to escape their problem they drive people away with their constant oversharing or cries for help. In the end, they hide the truth to guard their own hearts. They pretend all is well, that things are getting better. It's easier that way, and slowly, bit by bit, they become residents of the Shadowland.

Feeling they have failed somehow, they become masters at making excuses for not attending functions and eventually the invitations stop, groups they were once involved in let go of them, the phone stops ringing, and they slowly become invisible. My one lifeline to a better day was holding on to a deep sense that God saw me and I wasn't invisible to Him.

If you are a person who understands this place, I want you to know you are loved, you are important, you are special to God, and you are not invisible to Him.

I am so thankful too, for a husband who never gave up on me and never complained. Time and time again he would encourage me, even when I wanted to give up and die. He became my dreamer, reminding me of all the hopes and plans I once had for my life.

Throughout their younger years my children were like beautiful butterflies that flew around my bedroom and brought such colour into my life. They never labelled me the sick mother, but thrived and grew into amazing people and only ever focused on the great times we had.

But here's the thing: when I was well, I felt wonderful. Not so much physically but in myself. Even in my darkest of moments, I had the most wonderful experiences—spiritual encounters that I wouldn't trade for all the health in the world, and also moments of such hilarity that often I felt as if I was living in a sitcom. It was as if at times heaven opened up and a ray of joy would shoot straight into my heart. It's as if I received "the oil of joy for mourning, the garment of praise for the spirit of heaviness" (Isaiah 61v3).

In his masterpiece, *A Tale of Two Cities*, Charlies Dickens wrote: "It was the best of times, it was the worst of times." This about sums it up for me. As dark as the days were, the bright days were brighter still. There were miracles and moments that could never have been mine if I'd had the life of my childhood dreams. I have been the recipient of experiences that only times of being alone and utterly spent can bring.

During one season of my life, our bedroom looked out over bushland that was extensive and unchanging—except for one tree right in the middle. Every spring that tree would burst into a cascade of blossoms that was akin to a bright light in a darkened room. I used to stare at the blossoms from my bed each year and think, "Next year I won't see you, because I will be healed."

But it wasn't to be, not at that time anyway. Healing would come, but not yet. A few years ago, my sister Anne and I did a tally of the times I'd spent sick in bed. It came to approximately twelve years.

That blossom tree reminds me that people come in and out of our lives for special reasons. Chrissy was one of those people. I spent decades searching for Chrissy but to no avail, until she miraculously turned up in my life again many years later. Once again, she captured my heart. I had no idea that she went on to become a nurse, as did I. She also travelled the world and married, and had three sons.

Chrissy and I were reunited through my other childhood friend, Lynda, when we attended her mum's funeral. Chrissy was the charge nurse of the care home Lynda's mum was a resident in. That's when I understood that no one just happens to be passing through our lives. Everyone is chosen by God and loved by God, and their presence in our lives is for a purpose, even if we don't recognise it at the time.

I think we all have the potential to be a blossom tree for someone. Our abilities may be limited by our circumstances, but at the very least we can offer a prayer for someone who comes to mind, or send a text or make a phone call.

We all can be like that blossom tree and light up someone's life. Like small sparkles reflecting the sun on the desert sand, kind words, friendly gestures—all these are little things that mean a lot. That is what those flowers on an otherwise featureless landscape meant to me.

- 3 -

One Moment in Time

It was one of those spring days that makes you feel glad to be alive. The winter crispness was disappearing from the early mornings. This made getting up at 5 a.m. to get to the hospital in time for my 7 a.m. start so much more palatable. I was now a 'three striper'. For those in the know, this meant that the three blue vertical stripes on my nurse's cap would soon be replaced with a green horizontal stripe that would wind its way from one side of my cap to the other. After three years of study, work experience and exams, becoming a registered nurse was finally a reality.

The corridor in the respiratory ward of Wellington Hospital was long and straight, with patients' beds, a staff area and other facilities occupying rooms on either side. Wide enough to wheel food trolleys, beds and equipment, it was a spacious corridor buzzing with life as staff went about their daily duties. Shafts of light streaked through the windows, warming the rooms.

I looked at my fob watch. It was early afternoon. I was looking forward to the three-thirty mark, when I could rip off my cap, put on my coat, and run like the wind through the car park to my yellow Mini and drive home again. Little did I know that this afternoon was going to be different, and something was about to happen that would shake my world.

Standing at the far end of the ward, I looked up. In the distance I could see the senior charge nurse, whose job was to oversee all of the wards on the morning shift, striding down the corridor. With a serious face, she turned and went into the office of the charge nurse on the ward. There was nothing unusual in that; it was business as usual.

I was about to go to my next task when both senior nurses walked out of the office. Instead of heading towards the exit, they looked straight at me. Something caused me to stop. My brain went into immediate guilt mode. *Was I in trouble?* As hard as we student nurses worked, we also played. *Was it the wheelchair races? Had someone reported on me because I used the patient's toilets in the Ear, Nose and Throat ward, and instead of pulling the chain to flush the toilet, had pulled the wrong chain three times, signalling the code for cardiac arrest?* This embarrassing action of mine had caused the entire medical staff to descend on the patients' toilets, defibrillator in tow, only to find me, guilty and red-faced, coming out of the toilet cubicle.

What could I be in trouble for? My mind was racing through all the latest hijinks me and my nurse friends had been up to. But no, not today. Today, the charge nurse wanted to speak to me about something entirely different.

"Nurse Westerman, I am sorry but your father has been in an accident and is currently being brought here to the hospital by ambulance. As far as we know, he has serious chest and head injuries, and he is likely to be admitted to this ward. You may stand down from duty. Give yourself a moment to take in what I have told you, and then go and be with your family."

What did she just say? I wasn't quite sure. Her mouth was moving and I could hear words coming out but it was as if everything had turned to slow motion. *Think, think, what did she say? Dad was in a serious accident? When, where, how?* I was soon to find out.

༄

My father began his education in Holland but had to abandon his plans of attending a higher technical school during the second world war when the occupying Germans commandeered the school for other purposes. At fourteen years of age, he embarked on five years of night school and became an apprentice fitter and turner.

When Dad emigrated to New Zealand, he got a job working on ships at the Wellington docks. The hours were long and hard. Some shifts ran from early evening until 4 o'clock in the morning, but eventually Dad progressed to being a foreman in charge of a team of apprentice fitter and turners.

Dad stayed with the same company all his working life. For reasons he never fully understood himself, he even turned down a managerial position to continue working on the docks. Everyone and anyone who worked on the Wellington docks at this time knew the tall Dutchman. He was fair and kind, yet not someone to be taken for a fool and could stand his own ground in any given situation.

On this particular November day, Dad and his team of three young apprentices were leaning on the railing of the *Arahanga* ferry. Two tugboats were pulling the vessel into the wharf with a large towline cable. During berthing, one of the tugboats was in danger of being caught between the ferry and the wharf, and the tow cable was quickly released.

⁓

One moment in time can change a person's life. Our daily lives can seem so hum drum, yet we never know when that one moment might come that alters the canvas of our lives forever. November 6, 1979 at 1 p.m. was one of those moments as the towline unexpectedly whiplashed, hitting my dad and the three apprentices standing at the railing on the *Arahanga*. With a split second to react, Dad threw himself on the apprentice beside him—an act that saved that young man's life, protecting him from the full whip of the cable.

Also standing with Dad was another apprentice who was to be married the following Saturday. He took the full force of the cable and died on arrival at Wellington Hospital.

The third apprentice was injured, but survived.

My fifty-one-year-old dad, Tony Westerman, was the last to be stretchered off the ferry, unaware that he was about to enter the fight of his life.

Much of the rest of that day was a blur. My sister Caroline heard about the accident on the car radio as she drove home from Upper Hutt where she was studying to be an occupational therapist. My older sister Anne was living and working in Auckland. Never could they have imagined that the tragedy they were hearing on the radio was about their own father. This was before cell phones and the internet. Information reached the public at a much slower pace.

The following day, the Dominion Post had almost an entire page about the accident, with accompanying photos of my dad being carried off the ferry on a stretcher. The headline read, *Whiplash of Towline Kills Worker, Injures Three*. As a reader, stories seem so far away, almost unreal. But when it's your own family, it feels very different, very different indeed.

Back at the hospital, I awaited Mum's arrival and soon discovered that Dad was no longer to be admitted to the ward I was nursing in. Having sustained major chest injuries and a fracture to his skull, he was now going to be admitted to the intensive care unit. My mum kept a bedside vigil. The outcome for Dad was unknown; it was a case of watch and wait.

From time to time we hear of miracles, stories of such grandeur that to hear about them leaves us wide-eyed and amazed. But I believe much of life is a miracle, that miracles are all around us, every day. They often present in the little things that we take for granted—the right person being in the right place at the right time, a kind word when someone is at their lowest, a near miss on the road while out driving—little moments that could have such terrible outcomes but because of one small thing that could be considered chance, things turn out well after all.

Yes, much of life is a miracle, and I thank God for people who are willing to help make those miracles happen. For my dad, his miracle was about to begin.

My parents still attended the Salvation Army church, but it was more than a church to them; it was a family. As soon as word of the accident reached the pastors of the church, the phones started ringing. "Tony Westerman has been in a terrible accident. There are others with injuries as well. Someone has died. The side door to the church hall has been left unlocked so anyone can come and say a prayer for Tony."

And they came. They walked and they drove as one by one people made their way to the Salvation Army church in Tawa, quietly slipped through the side door of the church, and started to pray. That day in Tawa, as an ordinary group of men and women gathered on behalf of Dad, something shifted. We couldn't pray or even think straight, and Dad needed help in the battle as he lay in intensive care. Now, as my parents' church family quietly came and went throughout the afternoon, into the evening, and through the night, they held us up in prayer.

I believe when God sees us, He sees the bigger picture. He understands why we are the way we are, and He has compassion. He knows who we are, where we have been, and why we do the things we do. A lot of our behaviours are rooted in fear, as if our emotions are trapped somewhere in another time and place.

My dad had already fought many battles in his life. Sometimes this made him appear to have a short fuse, and he could appear quite driven, as I'm told many Dutch men are. But somewhere inside the heart of this towering strong man still beat the heart of the boy who was expected to be man of the house. His father had been forced by the Nazis into labour camps, and when he was sent to Poland to help build the Atlantic Wall as a fortification against the allied landing, my dad was left to work as stove-maker and care for his two sisters and mother. He was only a teenager.

One day, my dad and a friend called Bertus went searching for food, as starvation was knocking at the door. They took two old bicycles and cycled some distance away, diving into ditches when the sound of Spitfires was heard overhead. Along the way they sustained as many as twenty tyre punctures, but eventually they reached

Papendrecht, where they stumbled upon an aircraft factory. Inside, they discovered a building full of army tanks and food. A guard took pity on them and helped them gather some provisions which they then took to the home of a local resident. They shared some of the food with this resident, and in turn he put them up for the night. In the morning they went on their way with food and new tyres on their bikes.

As they came to the river Noort, however, they found it heavily patrolled by German soldiers. Sneaking past the checkpoints they found someone who would row them across the river in a boat for a guilder each. Once on the other side of the river they got word that troops had stormed Rotterdam and were rounding up all young men for forced labour camps.

At this point a kind, retired schoolteacher agreed to hide Bertus and my dad in his house. Unfortunately, Bertus was found hiding underneath a kitchen table and was taken away. My dad managed to evade capture by hiding in a coal shed where he remained all day. The next day he continued on alone.

On his journey back home, Dad was stopped by a soldier of the *Hermann Goering* division. The soldier was meant to capture my dad, but for some unknown reason waved him on his journey. Still, the journey was not over. Approaching the river Schie, Dad again found the bridges heavily patrolled. When halted by yet another soldier, he burst into tears, explaining to the soldier that his father was in a forced labour camp and that he was taking food to his mother and sisters who were starving. Once again, another soldier broke rank and gave him directions to evade any further checkpoints. From there, Dad cycled safely home with the food he had procured.

It was daytime on May 14, 1940 when the bombs started falling on Rotterdam. Dad was at the shipyards at the time, and all he could think of was his mother. He started running as if his life depended on it, which I guess it did. Running past buildings as they started coming down, past the screaming people who were running everywhere but nowhere, he finally came upon the apartment block that was his family's home. Rubble was everywhere on the streets, memories and broken furniture all tossed in the air before landing broken in dusty piles. But the family's apartment was still standing—and his mum and his sisters were miraculously safe too. That was all that mattered. They would live to see another day.

Now, however, my dad was fighting yet another battle. Thankfully, it was one he would also win. The day after the many friends and even strangers took time out of their day to pray for my dad, he began improving in leaps and bounds. It wasn't long until he was moved to the general ward, and then eventually he was sent home to recover. In time Dad went back to work and the events of November 6, 1979 became a distant memory.

The outcome could have been so different. Dad was the lucky one. He survived with the only remnants of that dark day the occasional bout of vertigo. We needed him. He had grandchildren to meet, family weddings to attend, and he also had more battles to fight. Mum would need him in the years to come, to care for her through the long journey of Parkinson's disease. By God's grace, Dad lived to a ripe old age.

Years later, my dad's funeral was held in the same church where many had prayed for him that day in 1979—prayers like invisible writing on the walls that have forever impacted people's lives. I doubt that many in the congregation ever knew of his earlier life. He was simply the man who carried his sick wife into church each week, and then in turn came with his own walking frame. Many only knew him as the elderly man who, with the help of others, maintained and loved the church as his own home.

All of us have moments when life changes suddenly. Events that were so pivotal and life-changing become distant memories in the fullness of time, but I still remember those who carried us and walked with us during those difficult days. To everyone who helped us during dad's accident and recovery, I have not forgotten what you did for our family, and to those wonderful people, I say thank you.

- 4 -

Oma's Song

One of my earliest memories is of my mother singing. I was standing in my cot trying to peek through the curtains as she went past the bedroom window. The laundry basket was loaded with wet washing, and she was holding it tightly against her chest. I must have been between two or three years old, which seems rather young to have such a vivid memory, and although the picture in my mind is but a flash of a moment, it is still clear all these years later.

It was as if my mother had a tracking device attached to her person. We only had to follow the sound of singing and we would find her. She sang from morning to night, and in between. Blessed with a pleasant voice, though admittedly not a voice that would make her famous, it streamed out of her like a bubbling waterfall.

One theme ran through most of her songs. She had many in her repertoire, but they were almost always about the same subject, and that was how much she loved God. Her faith in God was indisputable, sincere, and without measure.

My mother did so many fun things with us. She also helped me when I was too sick to look after my two young children. She was like a musical storyteller, an ever-flowing fountain of worship weaving around the ups and downs of her life.

Being the youngest of seven girls and two boys, Mum grew up in Holland in a home where beds were shared with her sisters, and compared to the Western view of riches today, I guess they didn't have much.

My mother's name was Hendrika, shortened to Rita. She was 'mum' to us, but in her later life when she became a grandmother, she became *Oma* to all of us.

Oma's own mother had been sick with diabetes and cancer, and she died at the age of fifty-eight, when Oma was still in her early teens. At that point, Oma was forced to give up her education to take care of the home and help support the needs of her large family.

During World War II, my mother was fortunate to have a job as a housekeeper for a family who was privileged, in that they had enough food to eat. One of her duties was to peel the potatoes. Each day she would bundle up the potato peels and carry them home where she would make potato-peel soup. Food was scarce and starvation was a reality for many in Holland, so potato-peel soup was a blessing for a hungry family.

Oma's family were not naturally slim people and even though food was scarce they never became skin and bone, as many did during the war. Oma had a lovely, curvy figure most of her life—that is, until Parkinson's disease became her reality.

I still remember with fondness cuddling up as a child on her knee at night, folded in those warm embracing arms. Terror would strike my heart whenever she would talk about going on a diet, as I was sure that she would somehow have a personality change, and that along with the weight, her loveliness would also fly out the window. I wanted her just the way she was, and that was beautiful to me.

Oma had two at-home outfits that she would wear—an apron over her dress, or her petticoat. On a hot summer's day when she came home from an outing, she would take off her streetwear and often just tear around the house getting things done in her opaque petticoat, all the while lifting up her voice in continuous song.

I remember how my heart literally stood still in my chest the day my father told us that Oma had been diagnosed with Parkinson's disease. I was frozen with fear. My immediate thought was that she was going to unravel virtually overnight and become incapable of doing anything for herself. But Parkinson's disease generally does not manifest itself that way. It's slow and insidious and for my mum, it would become a journey of many years. But I didn't know that at the time.

Parkinson's disease is a disorder of the central nervous system that affects movement, often including tremors. At this time there is no cure, but Parkinson's disease is generally well managed with medication. Lifestyle changes such as daily moderate exercise and getting enough rest are also beneficial. It generally only has a minor effect on life expectancy, but in the end stages it can be quite debilitating for the person who suffers from it.

I remember studying Parkinson's disease briefly during my nursing training. The only reason that this lecture has remained such a strong memory is because the tutor's explanation of the symptoms had been highly descriptive and rather over the top, and we got the giggles. Having sat for hours of lectures, my nursing student friends and I picked up on any excuse for a laugh, and on this occasion, our entire row got kicked out of class because of our rowdy behaviour. Happily, we got up and left and went for a walk.

Now about fifteen years had passed since that lecture, and Parkinson's disease was about to become a reality in my own family. My parents were about to leave a routine doctor's appointment when my father mentioned that my mother's little finger had started to twitch and tremble from time to time.

The routine appointment went out the window. Suddenly the doctor became very serious in his manner. He arranged an appointment with a neurologist and the diagnosis was soon made. Oma had Parkinson's disease.

That small trembling finger would eventually become like an ever-lengthening shadow that moves slowly across the grass until everything was embraced by its shade.

But it would take time. Mum was only sixty-six years old and there were many good years left for living as my parents learned to adapt to this unwelcome resident in their lives.

My father, who we called Opa now, had always been in charge

and in command of any given situation, while Oma was the cook, a spectacular one at that, and managed the household chores. It was fairly typical of the times they lived in. But as Oma's ability to perform daily tasks slowly diminished, Opa became the cook and the cleaner and managed the household chores. Opa faithfully fed, washed, toileted, and cared for Mum until his own health issues meant that he could do it no longer and she had to go into a care home.

In this upside-down world, people look at faces that are considered attractive, and fashionable clothing and fine jewellery, as things of beauty. These things can be appreciated, but true beauty and true love is what my father's caring hands were to my mother. It's the same with a caregiver who in spite of everything still loves a special needs child even after a day of tantrums and tears, or a parent walking around half the night with a colicky baby in their arms while they themselves desperately long to go to bed. True beauty is found in persevering through the ugly moments of life.

―

A number of years after Oma started taking medication to help diminish the tremors, the dosage was slowly increased. This in turn brought on side effects, including confusion from time to time. But the benefits of the medication outweighed any side effects for her.

In her momentary confusion she would sometimes ring the police, and on one occasion rang to report that a man was holding her hostage! That day, Opa's quiet nap was abruptly halted as firemen, with the police following a few moments later, came crashing through the unlocked back door to save the poor maiden in distress. Knowing my mother, I am sure she would have found it quite amusing if one of us was in the same situation and had done the same thing.

Opa had been caring for Oma for a number of years when she gradually become unwell with flu-like symptoms and a persistent cough that just wouldn't go away. Opa lived with an underlying fear that at some point Oma would be taken away from him and put into a care home, and because of this fear he was hesitant to take her to the doctor too soon and hoped her symptoms would eventually improve.

We also assumed that some of Mum's deterioration was due to Parkinson's disease, so as a family, we just accepted her decline and tried to help Opa where we could. Oma was, as usual, uncomplaining, so it was very hard to gauge how she truly felt.

It wasn't until one afternoon when one of Oma's Dutch friends popped in for a visit that Opa realised there was something quite serious going on. Sometimes it takes a person outside of our situation to see what we don't see. Oma was clearly very sick.

An ambulance came to take Mum to hospital. A couple of days later, I and my older sister, Anne, arrived to visit Oma, accompanied by our teenage children. I remember being in the waiting room when my father came in looking distraught. Opa had just had a meeting with the specialist. Oma, it appeared, had lung cancer and didn't have long to live. She was still undergoing tests but at this point things were not looking good.

My heart was filled with sadness as the realisation set in that she didn't have long with us. At the same time, a part of me felt she was escaping what could be an otherwise difficult future. Years of battling Parkinson's disease was now something Mum was not going to have to deal with.

The noise of the nurse coming into the dayroom to tell us Oma was ready for visitors brought me back to the real world. Gathering our tribe of by now rather bored children, we made our way into the cubicle where Oma's bed was.

Trying to keep a group of bored teens and pre-teens quiet for as long as possible was a mission, and I was embarrassed that we were not only disturbing Oma but the others in the room as well. My son Cameron, ever the showman, appeared to make it his mission in life to make his cousins and his sister Kimberley laugh. As much as it drove me nuts, I couldn't get too angry because in reality he was just like his mother at the same age. It was all becoming a little riotous when suddenly there was a loud "Shuushh!" from the bed. We all stopped in our tracks, startled. Until this point, we all thought Oma was asleep. She was most likely just hoping that if she remained quiet, we would all go away and leave her in peace.

Everyone stood there and looked at her, then went back to what they were doing but with a concerted effort to be less noisy. Soon, however, I realised she was trying to tell me something. I went to the head of the bed and leaned over towards her face and asked, "What is it, Oma?"

I can't recall if Oma answered me in Dutch or English. It's quite possible she was speaking in Dutch because no one else seemed to pay much attention to her reply. This explains a lot, because most in the room wouldn't have understood what she was saying, apart from my dad of course, and he was becoming as deaf as a post and was notoriously bad at remembering to wear his hearing aids or change the batteries when they went flat. As Mum's Parkinson's disease grew worse, she had begun speaking increasingly in Dutch. To this day I am thankful that my parents spoke Dutch at home when we were growing up so we understood her.

"What is it, Oma?" I asked.

"Listen! Listen!" Oma replied. "Can't you hear them?"

"Hear what?" I asked, slightly bemused.

Seeming a little confused that I couldn't hear what she was hearing, she said, "The choir, the singing, it's wonderful, it's so beautiful."

At this I stepped back and looked at her face. There was not a hint of confusion on it. I knew my mother's face and I knew her heart and I could see that she was truly hearing something of unimaginable beauty, only I couldn't hear it.

At this point she started motioning to me with her eyes. She was signalling upwards towards the head of the bed. She did this a few times so I looked at the wall but couldn't see anything out of the ordinary. I looked back at her and asked her what she was signalling with her eyes for.

She appeared momentarily flustered by my answer. This time she said, "Can't you see it?"

I looked again and saw nothing.

"See what?" I replied.

Looking back at me she said, "The angel, that enormous angel at the head of my bed."

Again, I saw nothing. It was at that moment I realised that my mother's spiritual senses had sharpened. As her body was weakening, the spiritual part of her was growing stronger. She was becoming aware of a realm that usually we are unable to see or hear with our physical eyes and ears. What Oma had always sung about with such passion and what she had believed in all her life, she was now getting glimpses of, and it was clearly something of incredible beauty.

The Bible speaks a lot about angels and their existence, but never in my life had I sensed one in a room or seen one. I knew from what the Bible said that angels were God's messengers, that they protect people, and they too worship God and do so much more. I also knew that the Bible speaks clearly that we as humans are not to worship them. I felt amazed and thrilled to be a witness to what my mother was experiencing.

Our visit soon came to an end because Oma was too sick for us to stay any longer. I was trying to tell Opa what had just happened but it all seemed to tumble out in the wrong way. *How could I put into words what had just transpired?*

Oma's condition appeared to worsen from this point and she was moved nearer to the nurses' station. She didn't elaborate anymore about the choir or the angel so I didn't persist with trying to get any more information out of her.

She had now begun to tell us each day that a man was sleeping in her bed with her. We would snigger and pat her on the hand and give her comfort in what we assumed to be delirious ramblings. Eventually she got so insistent my father reported this nonsense to the nurse. It became our entertainment for a few days as she would repeat her crazy story.

On the third or fourth day, a doctor asked to meet with the family. It wasn't so much of a family meeting, more a gathering in the hallway. The doctor looked rather embarrassed and proceeded to tell us he had come to make an apology to our family. He then began to tell us this bizarre story.

There was a male patient on the ward who had been there for some time. Part of his condition was that he had suffered a head injury. He was free to wander about the ward and he was wearing an ankle alarm. If he stepped out of the ward the alarm would go off and the medical staff would run like the wind and bring him back into the ward.

It appeared that this man had taken a liking to my mother's bed. At various times during the day if he felt a little weary, he would go into Oma's cubicle and slip into bed with her and have a sleep! How he had not been caught earlier was a mystery, but it became apparent he was doing this a number of times during the day. Oma was telling the truth!

The doctor looked serious. He clearly thought we were all going to lose the plot and get angry. He was greatly relieved when he saw our faces. We were trying to stifle our laughter. Poor Oma, we thought, but oh what a great story!

As a family we made our way back to Oma and apologised for not believing the story she had repeatedly told us. It was a lesson well-learned: always listen to someone if they have something to share, even if it sounds bizarre; you never know, they may just be telling the truth.

Little did we know that the medical staff were now questioning their original diagnosis and were considering a biopsy to investigate what was going on in her lungs. One day, as the family awaited the results, I came into the dayroom on the ward to find Opa, eyes closed, resting his weary legs by sitting for a short time. These days he walked with great difficulty. He often had to steady himself against the nearest wall with his hand as he walked.

Opa was long overdue for a knee replacement but he kept delaying the inevitable. He just put the whole business in the too hard basket. As a result, my father continued to walk until he could no longer function properly, then he would give in.

He had strength of character and fortitude in spades, but sometimes our strengths can become our weaknesses as we persist in doing things our own way. Eventually we become our own worst enemies and have to learn some of life's lessons the hard way. With Opa, his intentions were good but his body was under stress. He needed surgery and he needed rest.

That day, however, Opa had good news for us. Oma did not have lung cancer, he said, but a condition called pulmonary sarcoidosis. Sarcoidosis is a disease caused by inflammation. It can be triggered by a person's immune system responding to foreign substances, such as bacteria, viruses, or chemicals. It usually occurs in the lungs and lymph nodes. The good news was that Oma's condition could be treated with a course of steroids which would hopefully reduce the inflammation in her lungs.

Hearing this news was like taking a gulp of milkshake when you are expecting a mouthful of soup. This is not what I had expected. It was a shock to the system. Suddenly, Oma wasn't going to die, she was going to live?

I needed a moment to process this new information. Opa didn't look either pleased or unhappy. In reality I think he was just tired. We were all tired, but once the shock of the news subsided, we were happy, especially when Mum started to show signs of improvement and was transferred to a recovery ward in another hospital. Once there, she rapidly improved and was eventually able to go home. Her recovery was nothing short of a miracle, and during her recovery time in hospital Opa had time to rest and rebuild some of his strength.

Months passed, and Oma's recovery was startling. For us it was akin to having our mother back from another place, a place where immobility and sleeping was the norm most of the time. It was as if the years had been rolled back, and although she still displayed considerable symptoms of Parkinson's disease, she was much like she had been a couple of years before. It was wonderful.

I had mourned the loss of my mother as she had become a shadow of herself; now she was like Lazarus from the Bible who was raised from the dead! Opa still had to care for her, but he had his friend back and they could do things together again. Once again, they were seen zipping around the streets going about their daily tasks in their bright orange Mini. There was no stopping them. Even if it meant Opa had to half carry Oma into places if she was unable to get in using her walking frame, they let nothing hold them back. Oma's singing was ringing through the house once more.

Some months later we popped in to visit Oma and Opa after dinner. My family were all in the lounge with Opa, and I was in the kitchen alone with Oma. From my recollection, she was doing a small household task, something she could manage. It was so wonderful to be able to converse with her again and just enjoy her company.

"Oma," I said, "when you were in hospital and we were told you most likely wouldn't have long to live, I had a dream. I dreamt that you died and went to heaven. However, when you survived, I realised it was probably just symbolic, but it gave me comfort at the time."

Oma listened and then stopped what she was doing and turned to look at me. Wording herself carefully she replied, "Something did happen to me, but I haven't shared it with anyone. I'm worried people might mock me or just write off my experience as nonsense or delusional and brought on by sickness. But it was real, and because of it I no longer fear death."

I assured Oma that I wouldn't laugh or mock her. I reminded her that when she told me about the choir and the angels, I had believed her. I had seen her face and her eyes that day and I knew she was having an experience that was very real and very special.

Oma proceeded to share what had happened to her. "I was lying in my hospital bed in the evening," she began. "I was alone. I was so sick I could hardly open my eyes and I just wanted to sleep forever. It was at that moment I felt myself separate from my body. I felt totally myself and fully present and alive but I wasn't in my body anymore. Then I saw a great light, whiter than any white, and as it got closer, I began to walk towards it. Then suddenly, in front of me stood the most beautiful being I have ever seen. I somehow knew it wasn't Jesus and realised it was an angel. My immediate thought was, *But I am not good enough to be here.*"

"I hadn't even spoken those words," my mum said, "I had only thought them, but the angel replied to my thoughts and said, *But you are welcome in this place.* The moment he said those words he turned his back to me and started walking slowly away. As he did this, I felt myself being pulled back, and the next thing I knew I was back in my body and in my bed. I opened my eyes and saw I had a visitor."

Mum's visitor that day was a man Oma had often mentioned to me when my children were small—a man by the name of Lieutenant Colonel Standen. A retired Salvation Army officer, he was a man of great wisdom who had done many wonderful things throughout his life to help those in need. My mum explained that that day, he was at her bedside, praying. She heard him ask God to spare her life and let her live.

It was shortly after this man's prayer that an accurate diagnosis of Oma's condition had been made and the appropriate treatment undertaken. Sarcoidosis in itself may not have been fatal for her, but because she also had pre-existing medical conditions, her body at this point was in a severely weakened state. Without correct diagnosis and treatment, her life had hung in the balance.

Oma looked relieved to be able to share her wonderful encounter with me, and I was so thankful she did. There are times in our lives when it is right to cherish special experiences and keep them to ourselves, and there are times when it is right to share them with others. I was glad she took the time to share it with me. In turn, what she shared encouraged me and strengthened me in the knowledge that there is so much more beyond this life. Thank you, Oma, for filling my childhood with your singing, and thank you for your beautiful uncomplicated faith in God that became an example of love in action to me.

- 5 -

The Whistle Man

It was the end of a long day. Oma was in hospital again, and I had come to visit her in the evening. Life's pressures had conspired against me and this was the only time I could get away. I was hot and tired, but happy that I could get in to see Oma, even if it was rather late in the day.

Having spent so much time in the hospital as a nurse, it seemed my shoes had by now left invisible footprints along the corridors of the hospital. Laughter, tears, fear and joy silently echoed where many had walked before and after me. *If only the walls could speak,* I thought, *they would tell a million stories of the souls that had passed through these passageways over the years.*

That night, I was walking from one hospital block to another to have a meal at the cafeteria. I had visited my mother and was looking forward to having some time out. I increased my pace because there seemed to be no one around and the echo of my shoes and the wind outside made this corridor feel a little spooky. I'd always felt this way on this particular part of the journey from one building to another. In my sometimes-overactive mind I'd imagined that some ward escapee or a person with sinister intentions might suddenly appear, coming towards me. That never happened but I also wasn't going to linger and take my chances. I scuttled as fast as I could down the corridor and into the next building and made my way into the cafeteria.

To this day I cannot recall if the cafeteria was closed and we were allowed to use the seating, or if it was still open. I seem to remember that it wasn't too far from the morgue, and there were times in my past when I was nearing my destination or just getting a bite to eat, that I would hear the *clunk, clunk* of wheels bumping along, carrying another encased metal box. It would make me feel a little sad at the realisation that someone was going past me who had just left this world and entered into eternity.

But today I wasn't with my nursing friends, and a lot of water had passed under the bridge in the years since I had worked at the hospital. I was a mother now, a wife, and I had been on a journey that I had not planned. Who plans to be swallowed up with health issues—or any overwhelming life situation? No one.

When you are young, even the air you breathe can taste good. Gone were the days I could work and party and live on little sleep. Now I was bound to motherhood and marriage, and I guess, maturity. I loved being a mother and a wife and I felt blessed.

As I walked into the cafeteria, I noted I wasn't the only one who had taken time out from visiting to have a meal. About nine people were scattered around at different tables. Some were eating, some reading and others just chatting. I fetched a drink of water and sat down to eat. Apart from the gentle hum of people chatting and random noises from the fridge in the kitchen, all was quiet.

Then he arrived.

Unannounced, and like a miniature brass band, he entered into the cafeteria. It was the Whistle Man. His name wasn't really the Whistle Man, but that was the name I'd given him when I'd seen him parading around town.

Every town has its local characters, and he was surely one of the greats in Wellington. He would often be seen marching through town with large placards on his front and back. These were supported by a connecting rope or string over his shoulders. He had the wind-swept wild look of a man on a mission who never had enough time to look in a mirror or fix his beard or hair.

Whistle Man was devoted to causes. His banners generally warned that judgment was nigh and all men should get right with their maker or doom would overtake them. He announced his coming with a whistle, walking through town blowing on it loudly and repeatedly. He was often seen in the public gallery of parliament adding his weight to various causes that were being debated. He was loud, eccentric, and wonderful—all wrapped up in this person I called the Whistle Man.

People often fear what they do not know or understand. Sadly, this was the case with the Whistle Man. He was laughed at, scorned and mocked. Thankfully he lived before the days of social media as today he probably would have been eaten alive by internet trolls. As each group in society knowingly or unknowingly tries to conform to an unwritten code of acceptability, we can often make the mistake of deriding someone who is not like us in appearance or behaviour.

I'd often seen the Whistle Man in Wellington, and whenever I heard him coming down a street blowing away on his whistle, something inside of me stopped and paid attention to this man. Although his methods were odd to say the least, I had a sense that he was a sort of John the Baptist from the Bible who wore clothing made of camel's hair and ate wild locusts and honey. John the Baptist called his followers to be baptised in water as a sign that they had surrendered their life to God. He was also what people would consider weird, yet Jesus, who lived at the same time as John, said of him:

> *Among those born of women there has not risen one greater than John the Baptist.*
> *Matthew 11v11*

So, although I did not know the Whistle Man, I had a feeling he was someone who deserved respect, in that he was willing to be seen as a bit of a madman in an effort to get a bigger message across.

Meanwhile, in the hospital cafeteria, the Whistle Man had made his way to a vacant table and sat down. I pretended I hadn't seen him, as did the others, but all the while I was half expecting him to start blowing the whistle that hung around his neck.

But he didn't.

Suddenly he got up out of his seat and started calling out loudly to all who were in the cafeteria: "I can sense the Holy Spirit of God! I can sense when someone has the Holy Spirit in their life! All I need to do is shake a person's hand and I can feel the Holy Spirit's presence in and around them! If you line up here, I will shake your hand and I will tell you who has the Holy Spirit walking with them!"

Talk about waking us all up!

I looked around half expecting that everyone would keep doing what they were doing and pretend the strange man wasn't speaking. If anyone rolled their eyes, I didn't see it. No one jeered or mocked him on this occasion.

My instant thought was that half these people wouldn't understand what he meant by 'the Holy Spirit'. I mean, the words Father, Son and Holy Spirit are bandied about in relation to Christianity, but for some people, the only time they have heard these words are when they are watching television.

I think of the times I have watched murder mysteries on television. A poor hapless creature has succumbed to a murder and is being buried in some dreary (if not slightly scary) cemetery. The presiding clergy usually has the appearance of a man who has not seen the light of day in fifty years. He stands over the coffin as it is lowered into a freshly dug grave, his full-length ministerial gown gently wafting in the breeze. Usually, it is a freezing cold day, just to add to the appearance of all-encompassing misery. Around him, mourners look despairingly into the hole where the coffin is being lowered. The clergyman then calls out a depressing prayer that really brings no hope to anyone supposedly believing in an afterlife, and finishes it off with the words, "In the name of the Father, Son and Holy Spirit. Amen."

No wonder Christianity has a bad reputation for some. I would get the giggles sometimes watching these shows. It's all so farcical. But in another way, I'd feel a bit annoyed that it made a mockery of the most powerful of names.

The Trinity is not that hard to understand. God is three parts in one, just as humans are a trinity of body, soul and spirit. Every part has a different function. For instance, the human body enables us to smell, taste, see and touch. The human soul encompasses the mind, our emotions, and will. It is how we express our humanity. The spirit's function is purely spiritual. It is the only way through which we connect with God. We are three parts in one, called human. God, too, is three parts in one. The part called the Holy Spirit (or Spirit of God) teaches, comforts, and guides us, and so much more. He teaches us to forgive and love others.

Once again Whistle Man said, "People let me shake your hand so I can tell you who has the Holy Spirit in their life." This sounded like a bit of fun, and like everyone else, I was enjoying the moment. Much to my surprise, one person after another started getting up from their tables. I guess it was a break in an otherwise long day to have a bit of fun with the Whistle Man.

We were now standing in a straggly line with me at the end. Whistle Man then started to shake people's hands. Grasping the first person's hand he looked pensive, waited, then dropped their hand and stepped aside to the next person. He was silent and his face was serious. My heart started to pound loudly as he came closer to me. It was very quiet as we all just stood there with our eyes on this man.

In what seemed like half an hour but in truth was less than a couple of minutes he came and stood in front of me. Saying nothing, I put my hand out towards him. He gently took my hand. Then the strangest thing occurred. As his hand touched mine it was as if he had been electric shocked. He leapt in the air, jumped back and pointed at me, and began to call out: "She's got it, she's got it. The Holy Spirit is with her!"

It took us all by surprise because until now, while moving down the line he had been quiet. I stood there looking at him, taken aback. I couldn't find words to explain what had just happened.

The Whistle Man then shook his hand in the air and without a fuss went back to his table and started to gather his things to leave. The others seemed to mutter or giggle between themselves and go back to their tables. To most of them it was just a joke. I was flustered and was trying to take in what had just happened.

I quickly made my way to my table, gathered my belongings

and took myself to the nearest public toilets. I wanted to be alone. I needed a moment to myself.

I locked the toilet cubicle door and leaned against the wall and just stood there. It was as if at that moment God Himself had shown me that He was with me. I was a Christian, but in the day-to-day hardships of life I had lost sight of the fact that God is not dependent on how I feel. He is always with me in spite of the ups and downs of life.

Jesus spoke these words as He foretold that after His death God would send the Holy Spirit to be with believers throughout their lives:

> *But the Helper, the Holy Spirit, whom the Father will send in My name, He will teach you all things, and bring to your remembrance all things that I said to you.*
> *John 14v26*

It was apparent that to the others in the cafeteria that day it was all a bit of a sideshow. To them, it didn't seem to matter one way or the other what the Whistle Man said; it was just a little fun to pass the time. But it mattered, it mattered to me. That day, I needed to be reminded that I wasn't alone, the Holy Spirit was with me, He knew me, and He cared.

I never saw the Whistle Man again after that encounter. I've thought about him occasionally and hoped he was okay. Time has passed, and because of his age he would no longer be here on earth. Although he was judged by many for his eccentric ways and often seen as an insignificant man in society, I think otherwise.

Let us never judge people by their appearance, fame, wealth, or place in society, but by their hearts and the fact that everyone everywhere is precious and of value in the eyes of God. As I think about that day, I realise it was one of those moments when I was reminded that when we ask for a relationship with God, He is not dependent on our emotions. He simply promises to be with us always. We don't have to be good enough or anyone special. He wants to walk with us just the way we are.

- 6 -

The Dragon

As I write, it is a beautiful day outside. Our passionfruit plant is now dropping its fruit all over the lawn, and I can hear children laughing as they play happily nearby. I ask myself why writing feels so difficult. I guess I'm not strong like some people who can replay their dark times again and again with others. No, that's not for me; I've kept mine mostly hidden. Not because I'm ashamed, but because talking about it is like poking a sleeping dragon with a stick—leave it sleeping and may it never wake up.

Good times are coming, wonderful times, but they are not yet. To understand the present sometimes you have to know what has gone on before.

I remember the year we moved to a new home in a nearby suburb. Our previous house was a lovely bungalow that had seen over seventy years, but it had no garage, and the access was steep and slippery when wet. I had landed on my backside a number of times with a baby in my arms, and in the end we decided to move on.

Our house was like a shiny button—almost new, modern, and thankfully it had a garage. It sat proudly at the end of a cul-de-sac and was supposed to herald the beginning of a new life.

For reasons that have no logic, I believed that when we moved to the new house the hormonal migraines, sinus infections and surgeries, and ever-increasing hypertension would magically all stop. My children were now four and six and very excited to have their own rooms on a downstairs floor separate to us. We had grand views of native bush.

That's when I first noticed the blossom tree—I stood in our upstairs bedroom admiring the view and in the middle of the lovely vista was a beautiful tree, laden with blossoms, framed by all the green around it. Just as blossoms herald a new season, we were also about to embark on a new season in our lives.

I had slowly drifted away from my childhood faith over the years. I lived life pretty much on my own terms. I went to church with my children most weeks, clapped at all the clappy moments, sang the songs, and said all the right things. I talked to God when I needed or wanted things to happen, but the word 'relationship' was probably not the best description of my walk with God. I guess 'ownership' was more accurate. I retained ownership of every part of my life and fed God the crumbs. I was the type of person despised by many people—a hypocrite.

Meanwhile I was dealing with the billows of a life that was battened down because of ill health. When I went out, I put on the happy face that hung on the coat hook just inside the front door. I'd soon learned that continual cries for help don't attract many friends, so I would lie about my health and pretend I had it all together.

At home I did my best not to let my children see what I was dealing with. I didn't want them negatively affected by all the time I spent in bed or in hospital. We had a happy family, and Cameron and Kimberley were well adjusted, bright children. In hindsight I believe that God gave them tremendous grace, as they were really joyful, delightful, and seemingly untouched by what was going on with me. I loved them with a passion that only a mother can understand, and I still have that same intense emotion when even as adults they walk into a room.

⁓

Throughout my adult years, various people who have caught glimpses of my health's ups and downs have commented that it would have broken them. I have also been privileged (or not so privileged) to receive unsolicited advice from those who believe they are the fountain of all knowledge yet have no idea what they are talking about. Once, while standing in a church of all places, I overheard a gentleman telling my husband that if he had a wife like me, he would leave her.

The truth is, I could write an entire book about the absurd comments and medical quackery that has come my way. I was so hurt by what this gentleman said to my husband that I asked him in the car on the way home if he had thought about leaving me. My husband burst out laughing and said, "Don't be so ridiculous." Geoff has hung in there with me; in fact, our marriage has gone from strength to strength. My health has now improved so much that the memories of the ill health have faded. But the comments people have made still sit unforgotten.

Unforgotten, but forgiven.

Somehow, God has given me the strength and grace to forgive those who hurt me with their often-thoughtless remarks. If this hadn't been the case, I would now have a much healthier body, but my heart would be rotten, and I would be miserable.

As I reflect, I can say that my health problems did not break me. Sure, I would often spend half a day riding on a wave of self-pity when I was starting to recover from a few days in bed, but then the joys of living would roll back in the door and I'd be tearing around trying to make up for lost time and I would feel extraordinarily happy.

The year before we moved to our new house, something strange started to happen. It was like a shaking or a rumbling akin to a small earthquake underground. Yet it wasn't under the ground; it was somewhere inside of me. The rumbling would rise and try to make itself heard, but I would ignore it and turn my inner volume down. I told no one and continued on.

Then the new house distracted my focus, and everything was

about gearing up for the move. We arrived, moved in and it was wonderful.

But it wasn't long until I felt that disturbance again. Geoff had gone back to work. I had a part-time job but otherwise I was a homemaker. Cameron was at school and Kimberley at kindergarten.

While I was busy getting the family off to work and school every morning, I could rise over the inner shaking. But as soon as I was alone it came back. Each new day it got a little stronger. The shaking was becoming more violent until it was impossible to ignore.

Deep within me, a sleeping dragon was waking up.

Finally, after many months of suppressing and battling these strange emotions, the dragon awoke.

Then it stood up on its feet and *roared!*

The flames that came from the dragon's mouth were black, as black as death. It rode on my emotions and encapsulated all of me. From somewhere deep within, my spirit was crying out to my conscious self, *"I am broken. I am broken. Please help me! I am broken."*

I'd had moments of gloominess, sadness and depressive feelings at times in my life, as all people do. But never had I known such all-encompassing devastation. All was lost, hopeless—everything was hopeless. If I had been given a million dollars or had all of my lifetime dreams dropped into my lap, it would have meant nothing, nothing at all. Despair was my ugly companion night and day.

The dragon had finally woken up and shown its power, and I was a broken bird held tightly in its claw.

I became terrified of each new day in case the dragon was awake. Some days it appeared to be almost sleeping, but mostly it was awake. Fear gripped me. *How could I stop this unending pain?* I would have done anything to feel normal again but nothing worked. I dressed each day for my children's sake, but *what was the point?* When night-time came, I would have to undress again. I had no way to describe the intensity of what I was feeling. Everything was meaningless. I had walked into a deep valley. I had entered into what some describe as the 'dark night of the soul'.

I threw up my usual greedy prayers asking for God's help but I heard nothing back. I felt invisible, fragmented and alone. Suicide was out of the question because I wasn't sure where that would get me. After all, God might hold me personally responsible for taking my own life. I thought that maybe if I didn't eat much, death would come but it wouldn't be considered suicide. My thoughts were not balanced, they were loose and unchallenged and I didn't know what to do.

The months went by. My clothes now hung off me like a homeless urchin. It became obvious to those who loved me that something was seriously wrong, and they didn't know how to help me. My mother insisted she take me to the doctor. I sat in the doctor's office but hardly any words came out of my mouth. The doctor was so concerned for my life she rang me that night to check up on me and said she had never seen anyone that low. She gave me medication and I only took one tablet, but I was so knocked out that I couldn't care for my children.

I fake smiled, fake laughed, and tried to act normal when I was out, all the while trying to force the dragon back into its cave. But it wouldn't go. As Proverbs 18:14 says, "The spirit of a man will sustain him in sickness, but who can bear a broken spirit?"

How could a person who was genuinely happy most of the time now feel so lost and broken? Was it a delayed type of postnatal depression? Was it an accumulation of undealt-with issues? Was it some sort of evil power? Who knew? I didn't. But it was there and it was real and I could see no end in sight.

Somewhere in another part of myself, untouched by the dragon, I believed that God could heal me and that He was my answer. By now I was so desperate that I was willing to let go of my pride and ownership, and let God help me. But how? After living this way for many months, I had no idea.

For some obscure reason, I thought that carrying a Bible around the house might help me, and I guess it did give me some sort of psychological comfort. I didn't really read it, but thought carting it around might help. Looking back all these years later I can laugh at myself and appreciate I must have looked quite silly at the time. It was a pretty heavy book, and it's not so easy to vacuum with a large Bible under one arm.

～

One day as I was browsing through our local newspaper, an advertisement caught my eye for a Christian group called *Women's Aglow*. I'd heard about this group of ladies who came from various churches but shared a mutual purpose—to celebrate, worship, support and uplift one another, and share their experiences of walking with God.

I'd also heard they were holy rollers, that some of the women waved scarves around in the air over their heads. Apparently, as I was told, they dressed in long flowing skirts and sang weird songs while dancing and leaping over the furniture.

Sadly, the source of these exaggerated stories was other Christians. Humans fear what they don't understand, and gossip is alive and well amongst believers. No one intends to be unkind, but so often we speak without first checking the facts. When one group of Christians deride another, it's like 'friendly fire'. Some Christians are so busy shooting at other Christians they fail to notice that the world outside is looking on and saying, *"So this is Christianity? If this is Christianity then you can keep it."*

I stared at the advertisement for a long time. I took the newspaper up to my bedroom, and for a number of days kept going back to read it. Going to a Women's Aglow meeting would require stepping out of my comfort zone big-time. On the more hair-raising side, I might be encircled by a group of ladies who would dance around me holding hands like a band of unruly folk dancers and not let me leave when I wanted to go home. But it could also mean meeting women who would possibly help me and pray for me.

In the end, I just didn't care. I knew I couldn't keep fighting the dragon and the pain inside. If I didn't get help, at some point I would give up. Soon, I would have no fight left within me.

During this time one of the mothers at my children's school went for a walk one evening and never came back. Search parties looked high and low for her. Days later, she was found not too far away, in a local creek. She had passed away. From what I gathered, she had been emotionally in a difficult place. My heart wept for her, for her family, and for the fact that she could have been me.

I knew I had to do something. I would check out these women at Aglow.

When the day came, I was very nervous. With a glimmer of hope that change was coming, I managed to encapsulate the darkness within me long enough to get out the door. Wearing my favourite shirt and jeans, I quietly slipped into one of the back rows of the church where the Women's Aglow group met. Making note of the nearest available exit (in case I had to do a runner if the furniture leaping started), I sat down.

To my surprise, the ladies around me looked rather normal. There was a very pretty lady who appeared to be the leader. She was moving up and down the centre aisle saying hello and chatting with some of the other women. I looked down and fiddled with my handbag, trying to appear busy in the hope she wouldn't come near me. She didn't.

Surprisingly, all the seating was soon taken, and the meeting commenced. We sang a couple of short songs, and that was all very nice. Then a third song began. I saw a flash of colour at the end of the aisle and turned to take a look. There she was—a lady had got up to dance. Looking forward, I managed to sneak a number of peeks over to the left of me. I didn't want her to see me looking in case she dragged me up for a dance as well.

It soon became apparent she was dancing alone. It was more a sort of gentle movement up and down the aisle. Yes, she waved a scarf too—nothing wild, just gentle, and I began to appreciate that she really looked rather lovely. Nobody paid her any attention and it all added to the beauty of a lovely-worded song. So this was the band of weird dancing ladies? I don't think so. The outward expression of her heart towards God was actually quite moving.

Listening to these women, I was neither moved or unmoved. I was just interested. My heart was open, and I was not uncomfortable and didn't feel like heading for the exit. Without being told to stop, the singing just gently tapered off and the ladies took their seats—for those standing, that is, because some were already seated. It seemed that people stood, sat, danced, or did what they wanted, but it wasn't unruly. In fact, the atmosphere was pleasant and not at all threatening.

After a few announcements, a lady got up to speak. To this day I have no memory of what was said. I was just hoping that when she finished, I could ask someone to pray for me and I would feel normal again and go back to my life before all this hideousness began.

The speaker finished her message, and a call was put out for anyone who wanted prayer to come forward. The moment I had waited for had finally come, but surprise, surprise—I didn't move a muscle. Was I expected to march to the front in front of all these people? Yeah, I don't think so. I sat motionless and did nothing.

The meeting was now over and the ladies began heading towards the kitchen where tea and coffee were being served. At that point I panicked, feeling as if I had missed my chance. Pushing through the ladies who were heading out to the kitchen, I made my way to the front where the women I perceived to be the leaders were standing around chatting.

Gathering all my mental strength, I tapped a lady on the shoulder and said, "I wonder if someone might be able to pray for me."

She turned, looked at me, and I was immediately put at ease. "Of course," she replied with a smile on her face. She even seemed to understand that I didn't want a public drama and, grabbing a friend by the arm, led me into a small room away from the main church hall.

We sat on three seats in a sort of circle and I began to tell them why I was there. I hardly got any words out. I mean, is there any way to adequately describe the dragon? How can anyone gather together the hundreds of words circulating in this void called 'hell on earth'. I would never try to verbalise to anyone a description of their experience of deep depression. I personally don't think there are words in the English language that can adequately describe such a dark place.

The ladies prayed for a while, and then one of them said she felt that God had been speaking to her about me. I was excited. *This should be good*, I thought. But it wasn't what I had expected.

"Janet," she said, looking me straight in the eyes. "I believe the Lord—"

Lord. Yes, that word was familiar to me. I heard it growing up. It was used by people who had a relationship with God. It was comforting, and I liked it.

"Janet, I feel the Lord has been showing me that your problem is too big for us to deal with today and it's going to take a process. But I also believe God wants me to share a scripture with you. He wants you to remember it and read it in your own Bible and understand it. It's Ephesians 6:13-17. Let me read it to you." She opened her Bible to a section entitled: The Whole Armor of God. I listened as she read the words:

> *Therefore take up the whole armor of God, that you may be able to withstand in the evil day, and having done all, to stand. Stand therefore, having girded your waist with truth, having put on the breastplate of righteousness, and having shod your feet with the preparation of the gospel of peace; above all, taking the shield of faith with which you will be able to quench all the fiery darts of the wicked one. And take the helmet of salvation, and the sword of the Spirit, which is the word of God.*
> *Ephesians 6v13-17*

I knew that those words were originally written to Christians living in Ephesus, an ancient Greek city in what is now Turkey. I was a bit disappointed. So she wasn't going to pull out some Christian version of a magic wand and wave it over me and I would be healed? *Oh well, that's fine, I guess this must be the beginning of the so-called 'process'*, I thought. It was, but I had no idea how it would all unfold in the months to come, and although I wasn't sure what the words meant, I accepted what the woman had said.

The ladies prayed again, and to my delight I felt as if a great weight was lifted off my shoulders. That took me by surprise as they didn't say anything particularly spectacular, but there was power behind their words, and I could feel it.

Standing up, I thanked the ladies and made my way out of the nearest exit to my car. Arriving home, I felt like the old Janet again. Everything was brighter, sounds had more clarity, I could see beauty around me, and I was happy. I literally danced through my house.

I buzzed around for the next few days catching up on life. I didn't even have to wear the fake happy face that hung on the rack just inside the door. Maybe the ladies were wrong and this wasn't a process. I felt great! Hopefully this was the end of the dragon and the emotional pain it was composed of.

I mulled over the scripture the ladies had read to me but I didn't get around to opening my Bible and reading it again. I was too busy feeling free.

〜

A couple of weeks passed. My sinuses were still full of pus and mucous and resulting headaches were almost constant. I realised another surgery was my only option but even the thought of this didn't faze me. Life was good. I really thought the people at Women's Aglow had given me the magic bullet and it was over.

Then one morning I awoke, and the dragon was back—not full force but as if it was moving its tail and flicking me with it. By this time my fear of the thing was so great that the thought of the darkness returning was crippling. *Why, why was this happening again?* I did everything in my power to push the feelings away. But they didn't go.

The dragon, it appeared, had only been napping and now it was rising to torment me once more. My emotions plunged into the void of despair. There was no respite from the crushing immobility of my emotional pain.

Over the next few days, it got worse. A tide of utter helplessness overcame me. Once again, I could hide much of it from my family, but inside I was empty and alone. *Why had it disappeared when the ladies prayed? How had it come back?* It didn't occur to me that I hadn't done what they had asked. I hadn't read those Bible verses in order to understand them.

Over the next two weeks I sank. I was backed into a corner with no way out. This time I was mad with God as well. *Where was He? Why wasn't He helping me?*

It all came to a head one afternoon. This emotional valley was so deep I could see no way out. I bounded up the stairs to my bedroom and ran to the corner of my bed where I kept that big heavy Bible on the floor. Picking it up, I ran to the other side of the bedroom with the Bible in my arms, then I lifted it high above my head and threw it across the room with all my strength. At the same time, I screamed as loud as my voice would allow, "If you are real, God, then prove it to me!"

The Bible landed with a thud on the far side of the bedroom. It landed as if hands had opened it while it was in mid-air, then pressed the pages down. Expecting nothing, I went to take a look. Incredibly, that enormous book of thousands of pages had opened at Ephesians chapter six. There in front of me was the entire passage I had been given at Women's Aglow. I hadn't bothered to find the verses in my Bible, so it wasn't as if the pages had been pre-creased to fall open at this exact spot. I looked again to make sure I wasn't imagining it, but this was real.

At that moment, a calmness came over me and I knew beyond a shadow of a doubt God was real and He cared. He cared enough to show a hurting, broken person when she threw a Bible across the room that He was with her. I felt a presence, the presence of Love, and an assurance that somehow things were going to work out.

For the next few days, I read that scripture and thought about it. I still did not fully grasp it, but that was okay. I had peace. I read the verses again and again and began to see that although they were talking about wearing armour to protect oneself, it was actually about clothing ourselves with God. As I read about truth, righteousness, peace, faith, salvation and the Word of God, I saw that this was about a way of life and that each part of the 'armour' represented a different part of my relationship with God.

My perspective was changing. I began to understand that although we can pay lip service to God, unless we change and our walk with God becomes a true relationship, our so-called Christianity is nothing more than hypocrisy.

There was much more to learn and understand about this 'spiritual armour', but my spiritual eyes were now opening and I was gaining understanding each day. I began to understand that to allow God to heal my emotions I had to fully open myself up to Him. Only then would lasting change come.

Despite my newfound revelation, the dragon wasn't going to let go that easily. In no time its tail was flicking again and the dark feelings threatened to overwhelm me. I knew I needed to seek more help but once again I didn't know how or where. On this particular day, I took my courage in hand, hopped into my car, and drove to my sister Anne's place.

What she thought of me I can't remember, but it must have been a pitiful sight as I half stumbled through her open sliding door and into her house. Weeping, I blurted out some nonsensical story about how desperate I was. She didn't say much and I doubt if it made total sense, but what she was about to do would change my life. "I know a Salvation Army officer who prays with people," she said. "I've heard that God has gifted her to help people through prayer. I will ring her."

Anne called the lady, then handed the phone to me. On the other end of the phone, I heard a voice that was gentle, almost like a healing balm. I'd never thought about people's voices much before, but this lady's voice was like a river which ran with the softest, clearest water straight into my heart. It was as if love, like a hand, had reached through the receiver and was calming my soul. I was to hear that voice many times in my life. I didn't know it at the time, but I had just been introduced to someone who was to become a lifelong friend.

Introducing herself, Mel McKenzie explained that she couldn't come to see me for another fortnight but said she would say a short prayer for me. Before she hung up, she told me that a scripture was coming to her mind that she thought I needed to hear. She then began reading, "Therefore take up the whole armour of God, that you may be able to withstand in the evil day, and having done all, to stand. Stand therefore, having girded your waist with truth, having put on the breastplate of righteousness, and having shod your feet with the preparation of the gospel of peace; above all, taking the shield of faith with which you will be able to quench all the fiery darts of the wicked one. And take the helmet of salvation, and the sword of the Spirit, which is the word of God."

I could have dropped the phone to the floor. I had told her nothing and yet here it was again, those same Bible verses. Tears coursed down my face. God cared, He really cared! *Who was I that God loved me so much?* I felt smaller than a spot of dust on the floor, and yet at that moment I felt as if He was holding that piece of dust and cradling it in His arms. If I, of so little worth in my mind, was so greatly loved, then I realised that He loves us all with that same love—the homeless destitute, the outcast, the nobodies, and the somebodies. We are all *that loved*, not with a human love, but with a love that defies description and is infinite and accessible to all mankind.

I thanked Mel and looked forward to her visit. Finally, the day arrived. I half expected to see her turn up in a Salvation Army uniform, talking with religious authority. But it was nothing like that. I opened the door to a woman in her forties who had a lovely face and almost flawless skin. She came in regular street clothes and looked reassuringly normal.

We sat down with a hot drink. Mel wanted to know about me, and I felt as if she really cared. Her heart was soft, and as I shared my inner pain and torment, tears rolled down her face. She also laughed with me, and when she prayed for me, once again I could feel that same power I had experienced at Women's Aglow. It was the power of the Holy Spirit of God. I soon began to understand that God wasn't some distant being in Mel's life. He was her friend; she knew Him and He knew her.

As Mel shared scriptures with me I began understanding things I hadn't known before, even though I'd been raised in a church setting.

I loved being with her, and when she left I felt different. When Mel asked if she could come and visit me again, I readily accepted.

Every Friday for two years, Mel came to my home. It wasn't as if she had nothing better to do—she had the demands of her work as a pastor and she had a family as well. She always arrived with her own packed lunch, two sandwiches and a banana. She stayed for two to three hours, then without fuss she would give me a hug and leave again. She was humble and kind, a woman full of faith.

Mel was love in action to me. She would share things she believed that God had shown her about me that no one knew, and brought healing to the darkest of places. I learned that as Christians we need to learn how to walk in the freedom that God wants us to live in—that religion isn't the answer, but Jesus and His great love is. Mel explained that our choices should flow from living in His love.

We all have something within ourselves that others need to hear and benefit from. Jesus had His disciples, and He spent much time teaching them and praying with them. As we stretch out our arms to another and pull that person up into a new place, teaching them what we know, we are in fact discipling them. Through Mel's prayers, God brought healing to my emotions, but through her teaching she discipled me. This cost her precious time, and she gave me a lot of it, but it was time well spent. Slowly, the dragon was losing its power over me.

I was now waking up and looking forward to the challenge of each fresh, new day. I was talking to God as a friend, and instead of uselessly carrying a giant Bible around under my arm, I was carrying His love within my heart. I now understood on a deeper level that God wasn't a judgemental being full of religious mania and an attached prescription that said, do this and that and I will love you. His love was unconditional, unchanging, and pure. The changes I was making in my life were not to win God's approval. I now realised I had that, regardless of my emotions or behaviour. The changes I was making were because I loved Him.

Mel never pushed me to be anything other than myself. She never told me I had to join some religious group to continue my healing.

She simply came and sat and listened and shared and prayed with me. I went from strength to strength during that period of my life, and I found deep inner healing.

Brokenness and depression are not isolated to any race, religion, or type of person. Only those who have felt its power can understand the might of this dragon. If you have known this darkness for an extended length of time, my advice would be that you cannot do this alone. Reach out. Visit your doctor, a mental health professional, or like me, a trusted Christian. Your life is so much more than this valley, and there is much for you to live for. Seek help.

Time has marched on and now Mel is a trusted friend. We have ridden through many ups and downs together but always with God at our side. We can all be like Mel. We may not have the same set of skills and knowledge but we are always able to let someone know we care. You never know, you might just save someone's life as she, with the help of God, did for me. God brought the healing, but she was the vehicle He used.

It wouldn't surprise me when the time comes for Mel to go to her heavenly home, that firstly she will be met by her beloved husband Garth who has gone on ahead of her. Then she will meet her Lord Jesus who would then say to her, "Welcome to your heavenly home, good and faithful friend. You are already well-known in this place for what you did for others. Your reputation has preceded you. You are known by another name here in heaven. Here you are known to all as Mel the Dragon-Slayer."

- 7 -

An Inheritance

Before I trained as a nurse, I had a job working for an insurance company. One day, I went into the locker room to change out of my uniform before leaving work for the day, to find one of my colleagues in tears. As she shared her situation, I felt so bad for her. She mentioned that she knew a Christian who might be able to help her.

Grabbing my moment, I informed her that I too was a Christian and maybe I could help? To my embarrassment and horror, her demeanour changed in a moment. She turned to me with disgust on her face and with mocking laughter, she spat out the words, "You liar! You're not a Christian! How stupid. Don't talk rubbish. You are not a Christian."

Although she was laughing, she seemed angry. Her disdain towards me quickly overshadowed the problem she had just been telling me about.

~

That incident replayed in my mind over the years like a short reel of film. I was ashamed and embarrassed that she had acted that way towards me. I knew she spoke the truth, yet I was too proud to admit it. I felt intensely annoyed by her attitude. I mean, how dare she? I was a Christian. Sure, it was a 'secret agent' relationship that I hid from everyone except churchy types, but I was still a Christian. That day, I walked away bristling inside.

I now understand that most people, even if they do not agree with your spirituality or faith journey, generally still respect you for it. But hypocrisy is different—people see us as a wishy-washy nobody who is weak and not worthy of their trust. Most will politely not say anything, but they know. People have a certain amount of spiritual intelligence, and their antennae can pick up a hypocrite a mile away. No wonder my colleague had such a strong response that day.

During my latter teen years and early twenties, when I was living life on my terms, I'd held God at arm's length. I had fleeting thoughts about committing to my faith one day, but I wasn't quite ready.

How had I let go of my habit of sharing my life with God? I suppose these things happen slowly. Without conscious thought we let go of special treasures. We fill our life with other things, and soon there is no room for God anymore.

I didn't know that these moments were a great privilege and that growing up in a family where God was a friend was something that most never have. I took it all for granted—until I was empty, and nothingness was my daily companion.

Now once more I was hungering for the things of God and looked for ways to learn more about Him. When I wasn't at work or looking after the house I would hop in my car and visit a bookstore called Scripture Union. This shop is now called Manna Book Store.

'Manna' was the name given to food that literally fell from heaven which God supplied daily to the Israelites when they escaped slavery in Egypt. It wasn't as if lumps of meat and loaves of bread were being fired by a heavenly missile from some ethereal cloud in the sky. I think this would have been rather dangerous and slightly comical. No, each day the Israelites would wake up and find manna on the ground. It was fine and flake-like and the Bible describes it as tasting like wafers made with honey. It was picked up off the ground, and what was left behind would melt in the sun.

It's an interesting thing to view life from different perspectives. As a person who had always had faith but was now walking in it, I felt a little like a baby Christian. In some ways I was, and in some ways I wasn't.

I've come to understand that when you have walked through some level of brokenness in your life it can sap your confidence and you can correctly or incorrectly make the assumption that everyone else has got it together except you.

I had never frequented this place called Scripture Union before but it was a treasure trove of Christian books, calendars, crosses and wall hangings—it was all there. We were on a budget that didn't extend to book buying, but I just wanted to be where all this knowledge was. I took note of book titles and hoped to borrow someone else's copies, or get one second hand.

I loved the smell of those beautifully bound pages. It's as if books have a special fragrance—not like perfume, but a deliciousness that feels as if you are syphoning thousands of words off the page and past your olfactory senses and into the part of yourself that whispers, "Treasures, there are treasures within these pages. Imagine curling up on an afternoon on your couch drinking in all I have to tell you."

I wanted to read them all. Online books are wonderful, but holding a book in your hand is like caressing your dog. It moves, and the pages make a wonderful *swoosh, swoosh* sound when you turn them.

Entering into this wonderland of all things Christian, I felt rather nervous. In hindsight I see this all as rather ridiculous, but at the time it was a real thing to me. How do you act around other Christians? This was different to church or mothers' group, both of which had a familiarity about them. For some reason I assumed that the other customers were all icons of the faith and knew everything there is to know. Of course, they didn't—but the mind plays games, and mine would generally place me lowest in the pecking order of things. I would go to a book section and open a book, and as I read and digested the contents page, I would peek at the other customers. *Did they look serene? Did they all acknowledge each other as if they belonged to some weird Christian club? What were they wearing?* I even wondered if they all knew each other. In my own life I had often been asked if I knew Mr or Mrs So-and-So who is a Dutch person and lives on the other side of the country. I thought that was funny, yet here I was doing a similar thing regarding Christians.

In the end I decided upon a facial expression that would hopefully give me an air of holiness. What nonsense! In reality, it probably made me look as if I just swallowed an onion whole. I'd browse the books and light-footedly glide around the shop. There I was, facially contorted and doing a virtual hover glide around the shop, trying my best to look spiritual.

The silliness of it all! I was soon to learn that God has no time for anything fake—that being real is what He is all about. Still, I hope I never forget how I felt, and remember that others probably share those same feelings when they step into a place that's unfamiliar to them.

~

One day I picked up a book that looked really exciting. It was about a man's journey finding faith as a soldier in World War II. I wanted to read it so badly but looked at the price and knew I had better things to do with my money.

I was near the counter and had started chatting with the girl who was serving the other customers. I am sure she thought I was a bit of an oddball because she would half smile at me and not reply. Perhaps she recognised me and was starting to click that I was a bit of a window-shopper and wasn't likely to spend much money.

On this day, for no particular reason, I held up the book and said to her, "If I inherit some money tonight, I'll be back to buy this." I laughed half-heartedly at my lame joke and she smiled back at me. Putting the book back on the shelf, I left and drove home.

That evening, I was walking through the garage back into the house. Where I'd been, I don't know, but possibly it was just a trip to the local shop for milk or some such thing.

As I walked through the door, Geoff called me into the lounge. He said he had a surprise for me. He had just received a call from his mother. With a cheeky smile he proceeded to tell me that we had inherited money from a deceased estate within the wider family.

What did he just say? I was dumbfounded! I mean, it wasn't enough to go wild with, but it was a substantial amount. It would enable us to buy our dream furniture and a few other things for the home. We'd had no idea the inheritance was coming, and I was taken aback. It wasn't even the money that threw me. It was the fact that I had said to the lady behind the counter at the bookshop that I would be back on Monday to buy the book if I inherited money that night!

I tried to tell Geoff about the lady and the book and the joke I had told her. It all sounded a bit lame in the telling, but I knew that somehow the two things were related. It was as if I had touched on something bigger than myself—not a spiritual wishing well, but the realisation that there is power in our words to activate things in our lives, that God had given us mouths, and we can use them with great power to do good or evil. On some level I had always known this, but now I was seeing it play out in a very obvious way.

The Bible refers to the power of our speech. In fact, it says, "Death and life are in the power of the tongue, and those who love it will eat its fruit" (Proverbs 18:21), and that "gracious words are like a honeycomb, sweetness to the soul and health to the body" (Proverbs 16:24).

The Bible tells us again and again that there is tremendous power in what comes out of our mouths. When we speak negatively over ourselves or others, we need to remember that words are like seeds that eventually sprout and bear fruit in our lives, or our children's lives.

I hadn't grasped the full extent of the power of the tongue. I think the area we are strongest in is often the area we struggle with the most. Our strengths are also our weaknesses.

I was beginning to understand in a deeper way that to find healing in my emotions I couldn't programme myself with disabling words, whether in thought or with my mouth. Words such as, "I'm useless, I'm good for nothing, I'm a burden to others," had to disappear from my life and heart. I was being reprogrammed to be all God made me to be. It would take time to retrain my thought life—it seems to be a lifelong process, something I still need to work on every day.

The surprise inheritance seemed to indicate a correlation between my words and an outcome. Though unintended, it made me wonder, *Would the money have come to us regardless?* Most likely it would have, but God was using this event as a teaching tool for me.

That night I went to bed earlier than Geoff. The light of the sun had not entirely disappeared, causing a sort of twilight effect in the room. It was nice and cosy—mostly dark, but with enough light that I could still make out my surroundings. As I lay in bed, my mind worked overtime to try and process the day's events.

All of us have an inner sense of what is right or wrong, but sometimes it comes to us as a strong sensation, a gut feeling when we are about to make a decision that could benefit us or harm us. I call it a 'green light' or 'red light'. It's God's spirit deep inside us who either brings peace and confidence, or a sense of foreboding that we are about to make a wrong turn.

God speaks in a variety of ways—sometimes through that inner sense, other times through things people say or through a verse in the Bible. And sometimes He speaks in an audible voice.

That night in my room I heard Him speak into my spirit. It took me by surprise. I wasn't asking God a question; I was just thinking out loud about the money and the incident at the bookshop. Thinking out loud, I said, "Wow, was that a coincidence or what?"

Boom! The response came loud and clear: "Nothing is coincidence!" I am sure no one else could have heard it—the words seem to come from God's spirit to mine. But it was unmistakable. I lay there in stunned silence. I had heard the voice of God through His Holy Spirit, and He had answered my question! With one short sentence, my entire view of life changed. *You mean nothing? Nothing?*

My mind whirled as I grasped that we were all part of some great divine plan.

Coincidence. I spun the word around. *What if a 'coincidence' was, in fact, a 'God incident'?* The implications were endless. How I drifted off to sleep that night, I do not know. I started to see people and relatives and small encounters through new eyes. Bumping into old friends, being at the right place at the right time . . . nothing was just a coincidence. Everything was a lesson in the making—bad times, good times, even the worst of times.

Who would have thought that three words could make me look at life so differently? I was also overwhelmed that I had heard the voice of the Holy Spirit. If someone had preached powerfully on the subject for five hours, I could not have been more impacted than I was by those three words. It's true that God can change a life in a moment. His words held power. He had opened my heart to a new understanding of life, and it had happened in but a moment of time.

The following Monday, I went to the Christian bookshop and almost ran to the counter to tell the sales assistant what had happened. I reminded her that on Friday afternoon I said I would buy the book if I inherited money that night. I think my excitement may have come across as rather manic. The poor girl just stared at me. I hadn't prayed about talking to her, I'd just rushed in like a whirlwind.

In my mind I'd imagined she would throw her arms in the air with joy as I told her my story, and that she'd do a jig around the shop with me. But she just stared, clearly unsure what to make of me. I was disappointed that she didn't seem to share my excitement.

This was another lesson I needed to learn: gauge the moment. Don't talk rabidly—you might sound like you're on drugs. Be mindful of others—your enthusiasm may not be appropriate for their lives at the time; your latest revelation may not be the one they need to hear that day.

I left the shop a little deflated, but the experience was valuable. It caused me to step back and try to view situations from another's perspective. I reminded myself that I need to wait for the red or green light before I share something that I consider important. At the same time, I always try to remember those words, "Nothing is coincidence."

Nothing about any of us is a coincidence. Life might have dealt you some awful blows, but you are stronger than you know, and you are not a coincidence. You are a treasured, one-off model, created by God, and there is something significant for you to do.

So, look out for 'coincidences' and you will soon see 'God-incidents' everywhere!

- 8 -

Wheels with Wings

It was a beautiful, sunny Saturday afternoon, and it was all ours to do with as we pleased. Geoff was playing cricket. It was his favourite summer sport. Much as I longed to be an avid cricket fan, I found it wasn't my cup of tea and being a spectator wasn't for me either. It would also have turned into a very long day for two young children. Cameron had played school cricket that morning and was looking forward to an afternoon of fun. On this particular Saturday I had awful hay fever which left me rather exhausted, so I thought a drive to a park with a lovely lake and lots of ducks to feed might be the thing to do. Not too exhausting, but entertaining for the kids.

At seven and nine respectively, Kimberley and Cameron were a cross between best mates and arch-enemies. They could fluctuate between the two in less than ten seconds, and I was ever ready to deal with both—the typical life of a mother.

For reasons that escape me now, I thought that owning a sports car might be a bit of an adventure. We owned a bright red Mazda RX7 and had a lot of fun cruising around in it with our two young children seated in the back. It wasn't the newest model, but I thought it was beautiful and loved my little sports car.

It was a glorious day. There was not a cloud in the sky, and a gentle breeze gave welcome respite on a midsummer's day. We packed the car with bread for the ducks, jackets in case it got cold, and lots of enthusiasm. Born with excessive amounts of excitement in my bones, I could hype the kids into believing we were about to have fun, fun, fun, even though it was just a visit to a park with some ducks swimming in a pond.

As a child I used to drive my father to the point of exasperation with my constant excitement which I could never seem to contain. Even during television ad breaks I would have to get up and dance wildly around the room. Poor man, I don't think he quite knew what to do with me as he would tell me to calm down in Dutch again and again. It never worked for long and I would be off again prancing around being a clumsy ballerina or a famous pop dancer just like the ones I'd seen on TV.

I was now that same child in an adult's body, and my children hadn't fallen far from the tree. The three of us were ready for action and looking forward to our time at the duck park. My husband, although he could be a lot of fun, had a calming effect on us with his laid-back nature and this was probably a good thing. He stabilised us all in many ways.

By now I had developed a habit of saying a quick prayer before heading off in the car with my most precious cargo, my children. Basically, I thanked God for His protection and off we headed, the three of us singing loudly along the way. Little did we know that this was going to be a ride with a difference.

Halfway to our destination was a set of traffic lights. We were on a stretch of road that was always busy and could be hazardous—so much so that there is now an overbridge to carry traffic over the road. I assume the bridge was built because of fatalities and accidents that had occurred on this busy section of highway.

I slowed down as the lights ahead turned orange then red, and came to a stop. We sat at the front of a row of cars and waited for the lights to turn green so we could proceed.

It all happened so fast, too quick for me to take action, and anyhow, I had nowhere to go as traffic was backed up behind me. A driver coming from my right foolishly decided to run a red light and was on a trajectory that would result in him ploughing into my car. Short of a miracle, we didn't stand a chance. One way or another, we would either be killed or seriously injured.

Have you ever been in a position where time seems to slow down? It's as if your life is suddenly being played before you on a slow-motion camera. Ten seconds can feel like five minutes as your brain starts recording screenshots of the moment at hand with great detail and imagery.

As the driver came towards me, his car appeared to take minutes but in reality, it was only seconds. There is a song called *Jesus take the wheel*. In our case, Jesus literally took the wheels—plural.

Without conscious thought I screamed, "Jesus, help us!" In that moment, something unbelievable happened. Our car was lifted into the air, and it landed about two feet away! It's hard to gauge the actual distance but it was enough to take us out of the path of the oncoming car. We landed gently on the road just as the car that had run the red light zoomed past us.

I sat in complete shock. Did that really just happen? My children felt it as well. It was as if our wheels had wings. The car had lifted into the air and then been put down again! With immense relief and joy I kept repeating, "Thank you, thank you." I'd heard of divine intervention before, and it had just happened to us!

Snapping back into the moment, I saw the light was now green and realised I was blocking the traffic. Better hit the accelerator and get moving! As I drove off, I checked my rear-vision mirror to see if there was any reaction from the cars behind me. I couldn't see much detail, but I did notice that my neighbour who lived four houses away was in the car right behind me with her children. *That was a coincidence,* I thought. *Had she seen what had happened?* It had all happened so fast that I personally doubted it.

We made it to the park and had a lovely time as my children played at the playground then fed the ducks. Tired after a good day, we made our way home.

It wasn't until two days later that I saw my neighbour again. I was driving out of our cul-de-sac and she waved me over. I didn't know her well, but I knew she didn't suffer fools gladly, and in the past I had felt slightly intimidated by her manner.

Winding down my car window, I stopped to hear what she wanted to talk to me about. Excitedly, she proceeded to share her version of Saturday's events.

To my surprise, she had seen the entire incident unfold. She told me that she had seen a car run a red light, and it was heading straight towards my car. Horrified at what she was seeing, she literally froze in fear over what was about to happen. At that moment she saw my car lift off the ground and then land on the road again, out of the path of the oncoming car. "I saw your car lift in the air and move out of the way of that oncoming car!" she kept repeating.

It really had happened, and I had a witness who had seen it! My heart was once more filled with gratitude that we had been spared from something so horrific it could have cost us our lives.

I wanted to explain to her that God protected us, but by this time she had turned and was heading to her own car to take her children to school. I was a bit annoyed with myself that I hadn't used the moment to share God's goodness, but I hadn't, and that's okay.

I can't pretend to understand why God so clearly intervened to protect me and my children that day. I also can't explain why in other situations people sometimes do not have the great outcome we had; sometimes people die. I have no answer as to why one person may be spared and another is not. Life is a bit of a mystery. I guess one day I will have all the answers, but I don't think it will be in this life.

I treasure the fact I've been able to see my children grow up. They too now pray for God's protection as they live their daily lives. I believe miracles like this happen every day. Some may not be as obvious as ours, but they are still miracles. Often people are completely unaware of them when they occur. It reminds me of a verse in the Bible that confirms that we are under the care and protection of God:

For He shall give His angels charge over you, to keep you in all your ways. In their hands they shall bear you up, lest you dash your foot against a stone.
Psalm 91v11-12

Protection comes in many forms, many of which we are totally unaware of. I challenge you to thank God each day for His protection. You never know, you may just be surprised at what unfolds.

- 9 -

Love Conquers All

As Parkinson's disease gradually took over my mother's mind and body, Oma was placed into a care home. Opa had done his best to look after my mum, but he was also struggling with his health, and it had become too much for him. From then on, Opa would drive to the care home each day and sit with Oma until late afternoon, when he would drive back home for dinner.

Over time, Opa's driving got slower and slower. Sometimes, if the footpath got in the way of the car, two wheels would hit the curb and then ascend onto the footpath. He would then drive along with two wheels on the road and two on the footpath, all the while completely oblivious to the situation. Thankfully he wasn't much of a danger to pedestrians because his speed was such that even someone crawling could have moved out of the way.

Being the independent, strong-minded man he was, Opa was in total denial about the situation, despite the fact that his once-loved car was now rather dented and tired looking. It now sounded like a sewing machine that had got stuck on a bunched-up piece of cloth and was struggling to move forward on the material. The doctor had warned Dad to stop driving, but in his determination to be with Oma each day, he ignored the advice. Sometimes love blinds us to situations, and we unintentionally do things that are not good for ourselves or others.

Finally, I staged a covert intervention. My accomplices were the police, and the care home staff were my assistants. By now, Dad couldn't walk far without a walking frame. The frame was rather tall, and he still cut quite a dashing figure, even with his long, gold walking frame. How he had acquired a gold walking frame I never found out, but it certainly stood out amongst all the regular silver ones in the care home.

The plan was that the receptionist would call me when she saw Opa heading for the door to leave after one of his visits to Oma. I would then ring the police, and they would wait on the street to pull Opa over in his car. Then they would confiscate his licence.

The stage was set. All went to plan. Opa was pulled over, his licence confiscated, and a family member came to the rescue and took him home. From then on, Opa took a taxi to visit Oma each day, and he soon became a popular pick up for the local taxi drivers.

Over time he would tell me the story of the day the police took his licence away. He would run through all the names of the various people he thought had narked on him. I would sit there listening with a serious, knowing face, tut-tutting at the right times. Never once did he realise or imagine the nark was sitting right in front of him!

I remember the day we had a meeting with a geriatrician. She had come to Opa's home to assess whether he should stay in his own home or go into care. Our whole family was concerned for him at this point, as he clearly was finding it hard to look after himself.

My father loved the home that he had worked so hard to pay off and care for. I thought of the two young people who had come from the other side of the world and built their own little castle. They'd had a wonderful life within its four walls. It was more than a house; it was a safe haven from a country that had been ravaged by war. Tears and laughter, babies, birthdays and Christmases had all come and gone within our family home.

Some people speak of houses as bricks and mortar. That is true—but they are also someone's hopes, life, dreams and memories.

I sat in the lounge as the geriatrician talked to Opa. I was getting increasingly annoyed as my father presented himself as coping very well. He answered all the questions and seemed as if he didn't have a care in the world. At the end of the interview, he was taken to his bedroom and given a full physical examination.

I waited tensely in the lounge for the final outcome, concerned that he might pass with flying colours. I knew Opa needed help, but he didn't want to leave, and he didn't understand he was no longer the able-bodied person he once was.

We gathered back in the lounge room, and the geriatrician informed Opa, with guarded words, that he needed help, a lot of it. It was time for him to go and live in a care home.

Opa was understandably upset. He informed the geriatrician that he was not going, that he was not ready to leave his home. It was hard, so hard. This once strong, capable man was being told he needed to live with nurses and elderly residents so he could be cared for away from his beloved home.

One day we are young and life is an adventure waiting to be lived, and the next we are old and infirm, tired, and taking someone's arm to cross the road.

The geriatrician agreed to give Opa a bit more time and then reassess the situation.

It was only a short while later that God in His mercy stepped in. Geoff often went after work to weed Opa's vegetable garden, but this day Geoff decided to pay him a short visit in the middle of the day, something that normally wasn't possible during work hours. Opa, for whatever reason, had stayed home that day and not gone to visit Oma.

On his arrival, Geoff found Opa on the floor. We didn't know if a stroke had caused Opa's fall, but he left in an ambulance that day and never came home again.

During his hospitalisation, Opa's mind deteriorated and my sister Anne and I began looking for a care home for him to live in. I wanted Opa to be in the same home as Oma but we were told that it wouldn't make any difference. Oma and Opa would never recognise each other anyway, so there was no point waiting for a vacancy in the home Oma lived in.

My stomach twisted and turned at the thought of my parents

being apart. Even though they wouldn't recognise each other, we knew them, and they were our parents. I talked to God about it. I reminded Him that my parents had always loved Him and asked if He could please take care of this problem.

Incredibly, a space came up in Oma's care home, and we accepted it. The staff were kind enough to get a room ready for Opa next to Oma's and we were able to put reminders of home in it—photos, cushions, a radio, anything that would help him feel comfortable.

I will never forget the day an ambulance transported Opa from the hospital to the care home. My sister Anne had to work that day, and my other sister lived too far away so it wasn't feasible for her to be there. Thankfully, God had a woman by the name of Janet to help us that day.

Let me introduce you to my friend Janet Lister. Imagine taking a rainbow and plucking it out of the morning sky. It's been raining and the weather is bleak, and then along comes this rainbow and the scenery changes and you realise the weather is not so bad and there is still sunshine on the horizon. If you could take hold of this rainbow and put it in your pocket as a reminder that all will be well, then you will know what it's like to have a friend like Janet in your life.

I'd met Janet through a mutual friend a number of years before. She had come to our church, and I met her at the morning tea table—a good place to meet because it was symbolic of the many times we would have morning tea together in years to come.

She was wearing a jean skirt and nice top and had a kind face that was really attractive. When she spoke, it became clear she was from the midlands in England. She wasn't a regular church-attender, so this was all unfamiliar territory for her, though I didn't realise it at the time. I invited Janet to come to my home that week for a coffee.

Have you ever met someone that is innately good? I've spent a lifetime struggling to be the person I would like to be. But Janet was one of those people who seemed to have all the good characteristics that you ever aspire to have, as if it came naturally to her.

But Janet had one of those things missing from her life that you never know isn't there until your heart is opened and you realise there is a gaping hole in it. Janet could see that being a Christian wasn't simply a ritualistic, religious thing. It was about letting God into your life, and once your eyes are opened to it and you realise you don't have it, you are empty without it.

God was wooing Janet, calling to her heart, and she felt it but she didn't know how to reach out to Him. That day in my dining room, we prayed together. Janet asked God to lead her and be a friend, not some distant entity on the fringes of her life. It was a special moment for both of us.

It was now my turn to do what Mel had done for me. From that day on, Janet and I began sharing what God was saying to us in the Bible, and growing in our faith together. Janet's love for God was like someone who has found their long-lost father and is making up for all the missing years. She was unstoppable! Before long, Janet's husband Derek could see the peace and change in Janet, and he too asked God to be in his life.

Like me, Janet had suffered with ill-health. She had suffered for a number of years with fibromyalgia, a chronic disease that affects the bones and muscles causing joint pain, stiffness, and fatigue. Janet had lived with this debilitating disease and knew the all-encompassing effects of living with daily pain. It had affected almost all facets of her life.

Now, as Janet's journey with God went ahead in leaps and bounds, so did her health! During this time, she received prayer at church. Instantly, things got worse! The following day, Janet phoned her pastor and told him she felt terrible—that the fibromyalgia had exacerbated more than ever. The pastor was adamant that he had seen it go, and assured her she was, indeed, healed. Janet had worn splints on her wrists and hands for years. Without them the pain was unbearable. That day, Janet put down the phone, took her splints, threw them on the ground and kicked them down the stairs towards the rubbish bin. Instantly, she was healed!

Janet had walked with me and brought me encouragement in the darkest of days. She understood pain and its effects on a person's life when I needed it most. She supported me during medical procedures, and when I had surgery in Auckland she cared for me after an operation and sat at my bedside each day. Due to a detached retina, Geoff was unable to fly and could not be with me.

I can still hear the crunch of potato chips while having a lumbar puncture. Janet's concern for me resulted in nervous eating. It certainly took me out of my misery as I watched her sit beside my bed eating my hospital meals or eating a snack to distract herself from what I was dealing with. Oh, she made me laugh! She reminded me of the song, *Always look on the bright side of life*. That is the effect Janet has on me, even today.

―

The day my father moved to the care home, Janet was there, helping me make Opa's transition a little easier. Opa knew Janet well. In fact, he once suffered a heart attack and slid off his chair just as Janet and I walked into his kitchen to visit him. Janet caught him in her arms and gently helped him onto the kitchen floor while I rang for the ambulance. So, although my sisters were disappointed that they couldn't be there that day, Opa felt comfortable with Janet.

We later heard that the nursing aides who bathed Oma and got her ready for the day told her that morning that Opa was coming to live in the room next door. It had been sometime since she had seen him, and we had been told Oma wouldn't recognise him anymore, but Oma surprised the carers, and even though she found it difficult to enunciate words, she managed to say, "Can you dress me in my best outfit today?"

This took the carers by surprise, and they happily got her dressed in her pantsuit. She had loved this outfit. The pantsuit was pale green, soft, and lightweight. Oma had often worn it with a matching scarf and low-heeled sandals.

That day, when Oma was dressed, it became obvious how much weight she had lost. Once a full-figured lady, she was now like a little bird dressed in a large overcoat. Still, she looked lovely, and it had the effect of bringing the sunshine into the room. The carers did her hair and put a dab of lipstick on her lips and then assisted her to her favourite chair in the lounge.

I arrived with Janet a little before the ambulance, and we were informed that Opa would be firstly taken to his room and then put in an armchair with wheels attached to it because he was no longer able to walk.

As expected, Opa was confused and didn't understand why he wasn't being taken to his own home. As they wheeled him to his new bedroom, I could see how despondent he was and I felt like my heart was being ripped out of my body.

Eventually Opa was wheeled into the dining room and positioned at the end of a table in his La-Z-Boy chair. It was nearly lunchtime, and the aroma of roast meat and vegetables was swirling through the room. I was aware that Oma would soon be brought into the dining room to be positioned at her seat at another dining room table. There was no expectation of recognition between Oma and Opa, and I had been told repeatedly not to get my hopes up.

I was standing next to Opa's chair opposite the large entrance of the dining room when the nurses brought Oma in, and Janet was standing nearby. I looked up and saw two nurses, one on each side of Oma, supporting underneath her arms. Oma probably thought she was walking, but in reality, her feet were almost hovering above the ground. It was a tippy-toe walk, and she was looking down at her feet.

When Oma was about two feet away from Opa, she lifted her head just as Opa turned and saw Oma. What then happened took the nurses by such surprise! Oma, who ordinarily had little strength, suddenly had the strength of ten men. She lurched herself forward and out of the grasp of the nurses and threw herself on Opa. Opa threw his arms around Oma, and both my parents began to wail.

Now I have heard all sorts of cries in my lifetime, but never had I heard that sound before. It came from another dimension, a guttural wail of complete recognition, love, and joy as my parents were united! The most beloved part of their heart had been missing, and now it was restored.

They wept, we all wept. Oma and Opa knew each other, and they were in each other's arms again! Janet stayed to help get Oma positioned at the table, while I took my leave and went out to sit in my car. I needed to be alone for a moment. I needed to talk to God, to thank Him.

That day I saw the reality that love isn't about beauty or things, or anything that this world has to give. Love is from beyond this world and is greater than anything. If my parents' love was not diminished in spite of all that had happened in their bodies and minds, then God's love is even greater. God's love is eternal, unfathomable, never-changing, and it is accessible for all.

It's the truth! Love really does conquer all.

- 10 -

True Worth

I would love to tell you that I have a mind that only thinks good things, but that would be a lie. The truth is, sometimes I think thoughts that are best kept secret because if spoken out loud, they would taint all those around me. Thankfully, as I've journeyed with God, I've come to accept that He knows everything about me and that He loves me in spite of myself. He's after a relationship, not perfection. As much as we try to be the best person we can be, perfection is unattainable and an impossible goal.

One day I was visiting my parents in the care home when I glanced over at Oma. By now, she was quite small, in that she had lost a lot of height and weight. It was difficult to imagine that she had once been the strong, robust woman that she was in her younger days. It bothered me that nurses, caregivers and staff only ever knew her as this frail little old lady, so I had typed the story of the life that had once been hers, with a short description of her wider family, where she had come from, her hobbies, and other points of interest. I taped it on the door of her room and was told that the staff read it and used it as points of conversation with her.

When I visited, Oma and Opa were generally seated next to one another in the lounge room, and they were always holding hands. Opa was now thin and gaunt; although his large frame still occupied most of the oversized chair, his skin had the appearance of a tent that had slackened considerably on its support structure.

It wasn't as if he wasn't being fed enough. I had been informed by the nursing staff that they had been concerned about his anguish in the evenings. He would moan and groan, and because he could no longer fully express himself, they could not work out what was wrong with him.

One evening, a nurse came up with the idea that perhaps a man of large bone structure, such as his, required more calories than many of the other residents. The staff began to feed Opa another hot meal later in the evening. The transformation had been immediate. From that time forward, Opa was content and began to sleep better as well.

Illogically, I felt guilty about this for many years. The thought of him being hungry and unable to express that need appropriately tore at my heartstrings like a mother with a hungry child. Somewhere along the line our roles had switched; the parent and the child roles were reversed. I sat in countless doctors' appointments with my parents, made decisions for them, and watched over them like they once watched over me. We all had a role to play, and our entire family went about these roles.

Opa could still communicate with us, but Oma was now virtually silent and wore the blank stare of a person with advanced Parkinson's disease. Amazingly, there were still moments when her gentle and loving personality and cheeky sense of humour broke through to amuse us all, but mostly, she now had an almost expressionless face.

How can I describe this without sounding harsh? Looking at my mother, I had a thought one day. It was a two-part thought really, and the answer also came in two parts. Seeing the effects Parkinson's disease had on my mother's face, I thought: *Look at what this evil disease has done to her mind and body.*

Immediately I heard the Holy Spirit say in a voice that overpowered my thoughts: *But her heart belongs to Me!*

Once again, my understanding was changed in a moment. I was able to look past the ravages of disease and understand that our spirits, once opened up to God, belong to Him. Disease and death and evil cannot touch what belongs to God, and He guards this part of ourselves as His special treasure.

I loved my mother, so my second thought, although worse, wasn't so much about her, but more a general thought about people in her situation. I can't recall the exact words going on in my mind; it was more like a group of words at once: *She is robbed of all ability to do anything but eat, sleep and perform natural functions, and even that requires assistance. She is living in a vacuum, existing, yet not living. How can there be a reason for this?*

This time the reply came, not as words, but as a sort of revelation. Two seconds earlier, I had no answer for that thought. It was as if God had taken my head, opened it up, and inserted a microchip with an answer on it.

Suddenly, I saw my mother through different eyes. When she came to live in this care home, she carried the Holy Spirit within her! Her mere presence in this place enabled God's Spirit to move around the room like a fragrance, gently touching all those she came in contact with. In that moment, my finite mind could not grasp her immense importance in this place. I understood that her being there was so powerful that it wouldn't have mattered if she had been the prime minister or a street cleaner. We place so much emphasis on cognition and function, but in God's sight our worth is in Him. It's unchangeable and infinitely more powerful than we can ever understand.

I felt humbled and overwhelmed, and embarrassed that I had seen Oma as just a broken body that housed my mother who was lost somewhere inside herself. It is easy to skew so much of what is truly important. Whether we are sick or well, educated or uneducated, mentally strong or mentally challenged, when we carry the Spirit of God, He can work though us in a powerful way even when it appears we have nothing left to give.

~

It was as if a burden had lifted off me as I went home that day. God had not forgotten my mother or my father. They were carriers of His breath in that place and were still incalculably valuable in the sight of God.

Never underestimate your place in this world. It is far greater than you know! You have great purpose and worth in the sight of God. Even if you don't see it, God's love can work through you!

- 11 -

Till We Meet Again

Let me tell you about a man named Terry. Terry and his wife Raewyn were pastors at the church my family attended in my childhood. Now he worked as a diversional therapist at my parents' care home.

Have you ever spent time with someone whose life might not be anything extraordinary; in fact, it might be one of great hardship, yet being in their presence leaves you feeling enriched and inspired? This is how I felt every time I visited my parents. Many times, I would arrive to hear music that belonged in a large concert hall. Terry played the piano for the residents, and it filled the room like a heavenly nectar and literally took my breath away.

As Terry and I sat and chatted, I came to see a depth in this man that could only be borne out of walking through times of difficulty and coming out the other end. When he spoke, his voice was gentle and had a calming presence about it, and I loved hearing what he had to say. At other times, when a confused resident would be loudly telling everyone some fantastical story, Terry would look at me with a look that would send me into suppressed giggles.

~

I had developed a routine of dropping in to see my parents whenever I was out and about, to the point where I had become a daily fixture in the care home. It can be a fine line between regular visits and overstaying your welcome, and unknowingly, I had become an enabler, particularly after my mother passed away.

I struggled with Opa's obvious loneliness. But in visiting so often, I had allowed him to rely on me, to the point that I was preventing him from getting the care he was entitled to. I was acting more like a nurse at times, which of course in reality I was. But it was becoming unhealthy, and a lot of my behaviour was borne out of a sense of guilt rather than from a place of reason. In the end God intervened in a most unusual way.

One morning, I was sitting with Opa when Terry approached me. "Janet," he said, "do you believe that God speaks to people?"

"Yes," I replied. "I know He does."

"Well," said Terry, "this morning as I was having time alone with God before I came to work, I believe God spoke to me about you and I wrote it down. Would you like me to give it to you?"

Are you kidding? I thought. "Yes, please!"

Terry then gave me a piece of paper on which he had written what he had heard God say. I read:

Janet, you are a good daughter to your father. God is pleased with you and proud of you. Do not strive. You cannot control your father's life, even as he cannot control yours. Have no regrets. Go in peace from this place.

I put the note in my bag, thanked Terry, and went to my car. As I pondered over the words, I began to realise that I couldn't rescue my father and I couldn't be his nurse. Visiting him was the right thing to do, but I needed to let go. I was too involved. I needed to step back and trust God with my father. I needed to be his daughter once more and live my own life. It was time to look after myself, visit a little less, and take care of my own family.

It was like being set free from a prison of my own making. God in His mercy had spoken to me through Terry and thrown open the doors. I began to live again, and I also began to enjoy my dad in a new way, a healthy way.

Sadly, Terry never lived into old age, but my guess is he is now playing a heavenly grand piano accompanied by an equally spectacular orchestra. This time, his audience is not only the once-infirm and elderly who are now healed, but God Himself who is enjoying his music.

My wider family was a small group because all my cousins, aunt and uncles lived in Holland. Here in New Zealand, my sisters had married, and their spouses, as well as my husband, became like sons to my parents.

I want to share with you a little about my nieces and nephews. I have five of them on my side of the family and more if you include their spouses. Now here is a peculiar thing, a true-life mystery: somehow, I have ended up with the best nieces and nephews in the world. I don't know how it happened, but there it is. Some would say I have rose-tinted glasses but I know the truth and we will leave it at that. I also have nieces and nephews on Geoff's side of the family, who are just as special to me.

It was a Tuesday afternoon, and my niece, Melinda, who was then in her early twenties, was visiting Opa. Melinda is my sister Anne's daughter. The first thing anyone would notice about Melinda is her beautiful complexion and thick luxurious hair. But for me, it's her infectious laughter that lilts and rolls and always makes me feel good whenever I am around her.

On this particular afternoon, Melinda and Opa were hanging out together, enjoying each other's company. Opa was quite confused a lot of the time and Melinda knew to expect that. Then, out of the blue, Opa asked Melinda what day it was. Melinda replied that it was Tuesday afternoon. Then, quite matter-of-fact, Opa said, "This time next week I will be in heaven with Oma."

Not sure what to make of that statement, Melinda just kept chatting, and stayed with Opa until it was time to go home. She shared with her mum and me what Opa had said. Anne suggested it could have been a statement borne out of confusion. She also told Melinda not to write the comment off, as sometimes people nearing the end of their journey seem to have insight about their time and when it is near.

The following Tuesday morning, I was heading to the shops to buy a few things we needed. It had been a busy weekend. My sister Caroline, from Christchurch, had been spending time with us. Opa had taken a tumble earlier in the week and cut his head, which required sutures. Following this incident, he had gone downhill and was now suffering with pneumonia. Caroline had spent the weekend at his bedside in the care home, singing to him and just keeping him company. She had returned home to Christchurch on the Monday.

We were told that Opa may recover, or it could go the other way. Opa always recovered. He faced infections and accidents like bumps in the road, so we hoped that this time it would be the same.

That morning, just before nine, I was driving along the highway when for some unknown reason I changed my plans. I decided to go and visit Opa first and then do my shopping later.

I walked down the corridor to Opa's room. Linen skips lined the hallway, and caregivers, nurses and cleaners were like bees busily buzzing around in a hive. It was a lovely day outside, and I felt light and happy.

As I turned to enter Opa's room, I walked straight into a caregiver. We almost touched faces as we collided with each other. She grabbed my arm and manoeuvred me so that I was now standing with my back against the railing along the wall in the corridor. My mind was empty, and I had no thought about why she was doing this. She then closed the door to Opa's room and went to fetch a nurse. Still I was ignorant about what was going on. The nurse and the carer then went into his room and left me outside.

I waited a few minutes, and then they came out of his room. As soon as I saw the nurse's face, I knew. *How had I not clicked before?* I looked her straight in the eyes and listened to what she had to say. Opa was gone. Thirty seconds before I arrived, he had gently slipped away. Would I like to be alone with him? *Yes, yes I would.* Then I would contact my sisters.

It was now hours short of being a week since Opa had told

Melinda that in a week he would be in heaven with Oma. He was right, but how did he know? I guess that was between him and God.

I walked into Opa's room and closed the door. It had only been minutes and I was sure I could still feel his presence in the room. I went to his bed and cradled his head in my hands. My tears began to fall onto his face and then run down his cheeks and onto the bed. His skin was still warm to the touch and it was hard to believe he had actually gone. I sat there, on the edge of his bed, not really knowing what to do. No one gives you a manual for times such as this.

It was at that moment I heard a sound. Strange as it may seem, I heard the sound of myself speaking. I know that God sometimes speaks through other people, but this time it was happening to me. It wasn't as if I was a robot, or under some other-worldly control. It was more a case of having no thought process before the words came out of my mouth.

I listened to what I was saying. "Opa," I said. "Opa, I am coming. I am coming, but not yet. I cannot come yet because I have work to do. Then I will come, but the time is not yet."

It was then I felt a presence in the room. Not the presence of Opa, but another presence. I cannot adequately describe that moment, but it felt as if that small room in the care home had become a holy place, a cathedral of such beauty it had no equal in this dark world. I saw nothing but sensed something so beautiful I dared not move. Was it the Holy Spirit? Was it an angel? I didn't know but I knew it was there.

Then it was gone. The warmth of Opa, the sense he was still there and that holy presence, it was all gone. I was alone in a little room, and in the bed lay the body that once housed my father.

I was aware that something wonderful had just happened. I was also aware that I had to tell my family that Opa had gone.

I sat in my car and called my sister Caroline in Christchurch, then drove to my sister Anne's workplace to tell her. I contacted my children and my husband as well.

Anne came back to the care home with me in my car. We sat in silence as I drove. Here we were, adults with our own families, so how was it that I now felt like an orphan? It made no sense, but that is how I felt at that moment.

The staff had been very busy while I had gone to get my sister. Opa's bed had been repositioned along another wall under a window. He had been washed, and fresh, white linen was now on the bed. The rest of the furniture and Opa's personal things had been cleared away, so the room seemed empty apart from the bed he lay in.

We stood silently next to each other staring at our dad. Only his face was showing, and on the sheet that covered his chest, a long-stemmed, red rose had been placed over his heart.

Here we were, a couple of middle-aged women, but in that moment, we were little girls once more. The door to the room opened, and I turned to see who it was. To my surprise, it was my son, Cameron. I was pleased to see him.

Cameron made his way across the room. Without a word, he stood between us and put his arms around our shoulders. Somehow, he understood that we both felt lost and needed his strength. Then Cameron started to pray. It wasn't at all religious, or said with pomp and flowery language. It was a prayer of gratitude to God for the life of Opa.

I looked at my son. The boy was now a man and was taking care of his mum and aunt. It was a lovely moment, and I appreciated that he was there for us.

The following days were filled with preparations for Opa's funeral. Geoff and I had recently sold our house, and Cameron had been living in Opa's house while he was in care. So the tide had turned, and Cameron kindly allowed two new flatmates to come and stay with him while we were looking for a new home.

~

On the morning of the funeral, we sat around the dining room table eating breakfast. Cameron had a large poster stuck to the side of the fridge. It was a picture of Arnold Schwarzenegger and advertised his famous movie, *The Terminator*. The Terminator had been a box-office hit and was particularly famous for Arnold Schwarzenegger's one liner, "I'll be back." Arnold is Austrian, and his large stature, combined with a deep voice and strong accent, makes the words sound even more powerful and rather fantastic.

We were eating breakfast and sharing stories about Opa and his life. It was at that point one of us commented on the poster. It was joked that if Opa, who could sound a lot like Arnie (as my kids called him), had been given the opportunity for a final few words, he would probably have repeated that now famous line, "I'll be back!"

It didn't make a lot of sense, but it made us all laugh because we all realised how Opa's accent sometimes made him sound like Arnie. It was all said in jest and meant in fondness as we prepared to farewell him that day.

As a family we had made the decision not to go to the crematorium with the hearse. There would be a lot of visitors at the funeral, and we decided that we would stay back and have something to eat and drink with them at the church following the service.

When the funeral was over, my husband and I stood outside my parents' family church. For over fifty years they had worshipped at the Salvation Army in Tawa and seen births, weddings and deaths in this place.

The white hearse was parked in front of us. I stood on the footpath feeling rather torn inside. I wanted at that moment to escort his earthly vessel on its final journey, but also realised it was the right thing to stay back and chat to visitors, some of whom had travelled quite a distance.

Then, out of the church came the Salvation Army officer who had presided over the funeral. Often when I arrived to visit my parents at the care home, she would be there. Judith Bennett, along with her husband David, had been wonderful to my parents, and as a family we were so grateful for all they had done for Mum and Dad.

Judith took one look at my face and said she would go in the hearse with Opa to the crematorium. Then she would make her way back to join us at the church. I was relieved and pleased with her kind offer.

Now, of course, Judith had no inkling of our family conversation at breakfast that morning. She had no idea that we had chatted and laughed about Arnold Schwarzenegger or commented that Opa's parting words would have been Arnie's famous one liner, "I'll be back."

As the hearse started to pull slowly away, the front passenger door suddenly flung open. It was Judith. Leaning out of the now half-open car door, she called out to us loud and clear, "I'll be back!"

We both froze. What did she just say?! Geoff and I looked at each other and then collapsed with laughter. Was God having a joke with us? It was wonderful. I had cried so much that week, and now the laughter was a blessed respite. Sure, Opa was never going to call out those words from the grave, but the fact that Judith did from the very hearse that was carrying his body was nothing short of hilarious.

That special moment brought home the reality that we are part of something so much bigger than ourselves. That life, laughter and tears are all part of this crazy journey, and we are not alone in it. That there is a God—not some old stooge sitting around making judgements and beating us around the head with punishment for our wrongdoings, but a loving God who is part of everything in our lives, the good, the bad and the ugly. That He has a sense of humour and that there is a purpose for our lives.

Unlike Arnold Schwarzenegger's famous words, I don't think Opa will be back. But I will see him again, and precious others who have left before me. I'm so glad I am on this journey with God and I look forward to what lies ahead. As I said to Opa that day, "I am coming, I am coming, but not yet. I cannot come yet because I have work to do. Then I will come, but the time is not yet."

It is the same for you. There is work for you to do. As long as there is breath in your lungs, there is a purpose and a plan for your life. Will you choose to live with God at your side or without? It's up to you.

- 12 -

Be Yourself

A few years before my dad died, I had enrolled in a ministry school. For the next three years, I would join the class every Thursday night at our local church.

Let me introduce you to a lady who attended the school with me. She was everything that I felt I wasn't. She wore immaculate, corporate-style clothing of the finest quality. Her makeup was lovely, and her hair coiffured to perfection. She had an air of gracefulness and sophistication about her that I admired.

One Thursday evening I arrived in class a little early and spotted an empty chair beside her. Sitting down next to her and proceeding to make polite conversation, I asked her how her week was going.

She looked at me serenely and replied in a voice barely above a whisper, "I am doing my best to live as a godly woman, such as the Bible talks about."

Perplexed, I pressed her for more information.

"Well," she replied, clearly building up to some inner spiritual key I knew nothing about, "the godly women of the Bible never spoke much, they were gentle, subservient and peaceable at all times. So I am no longer speaking much, and when I do it will be soft and gentle just like the women of biblical times."

Well now, that was fascinating. I had never heard this spin on the way godly women were supposed to behave. I recognised that the words she used were pulled out of various Bible verses, but here they were being moulded together into the same context, a bit like a spiritual mashed potato. Without having the nous to go and do a search of the Bible for myself, I just believed her.

At the time, God was still working away in the background on my self-esteem, and I ran with this altered version of the truth just because I admired the lady and had no doubt she knew what she was talking about.

So there she sat all evening, barely speaking, a gentle, Mona Lisa smile on her face. After class it seemed she was almost floating as she walked out of the room. I would have to try harder. I would curb my excessive laughter, keep my mouth shut, and become the angelic person God clearly wanted me to be. I had to be more like her.

Over the following days I hardly spoke, and walked around slavishly expressing no opinion about anything and oozing humbleness wherever I went. I thought I would start to feel good about my effort to be a so-called godly woman, but the exact opposite began to happen. I started to feel miserable. I became grumpy inside and agitated at everything around me. My face did not wear the sweetness of a Mona Lisa smile. I looked as if I spent the day sucking on sour lollies until I had the appearance of an angry lady you would want to avoid.

By the time the following Thursday rolled around I was definitely not a Godly woman of biblical times. I was down, unhappy, and felt I had failed.

That night we had a guest speaker, which was always interesting as they brought fresh perspectives and built on what we had learned. I don't remember his name and I don't even remember what he looked like. But I remember that night as a night of liberation for me.

The lovely lady was there, looking happy and peaceful and together. Maybe she was, or maybe she was just a better actor than me. I tried to pretend I was all of those things but inside I felt out of kilter, annoyed and unhappy. I mean, I had hardly spoken a word in a week—possibly a blessed relief for many, but agony for me.

By now, I was full of self-condemnation at my failure to be the person I aspired to be, and my glumness was going to cost me friends if I didn't pull myself together.

At some point in the evening, the guest speaker stopped speaking. He began to scan the class. Everyone looked up to see why he had stopped talking. His eyes then fell on me. *Yikes*, I thought. *Why is he looking at me?*

He then proceeded to point me out in front of the entire class and asked me to come forward. I dutifully made my way to where he was standing.

Now, this man did not know me, and I had never seen him before that night. I had not shared with anyone the journey I had taken myself on to be what I considered a 'godly woman'. So when he spoke I knew he was sharing something straight from the Holy Spirit. He began with a question.

"What would happen if you took a bottle of fizzy drink and you shook it, then opened it?"

"The drink would come bubbling out and I guess it would be like a fizzy fountain," I answered.

"Correct," he replied, "and that is the personality God has given you! Stop trying to be someone you are not made to be, and be yourself!"

My mouth dropped open. *What?! God had actually made me this way—an excitable chatterbox?* This was the best news I'd ever heard! I wanted to dance. I felt free! I thought of all the times I'd disliked myself because I felt I was just annoying. I knew that at times I needed to curb the excesses of my nature, but I had just been given permission to be myself! At that moment I felt such great relief. In less than a minute, all the heaviness of trying to be someone else just fell off. I nearly danced to my seat. It took great effort to sit through the rest of the night and keep quiet. I couldn't wait to go home and be the mum and wife that my family had always loved and accepted. They didn't want me any other way.

That lesson gave me a fresh perspective on life. We have to let people be who they are. We have to stop trying to change others into something that we think is normal and acceptable. We must also stop trying to force our children into a mould so they will be just like us.

Quiet is okay, chatty is okay, serious is okay, being a jokester is okay. It's all okay!

So if, like me, you struggle with your nature at times, don't! You are awesome just the way you are.

You have permission to be yourself!

- 13 -

Simon

I remember inviting a trainee pastor to my house for lunch after church one day. The poor man and his wife were probably looking forward to a good roast dinner and dessert and a quiet sit-down for the afternoon. I'm embarrassed to say that as soon as they had eaten, I produced a written list of theological questions that I'd hoped they could answer for me.

For context, I was in a season of life where I had tasted a little of what was out there in the world of Christian resources, and now I couldn't get enough. I digested books like food. I would read and reread paragraphs so I could take in the fullness of what was being said. I joined an audiobook library and loved listening to stories retold by the very people who had experienced them—stories of overcoming hardships, and of miracles that I never knew happened outside of biblical times, stories of prayers that had such dramatic answers that I came to understand that wars were won, evil was overcome and the course of history itself was changed, all because people prayed.

My mind and heart opened to a world of unsung heroes who impacted lives on a daily basis—where nuns and monks literally changed the course of history while on their knees, cloistered away in prayer; where people from different arms of the Christian faith risked their lives daily to feed the poor, sit with the broken, and nurse the dying in their arms. It was like a million fires all over the world that couldn't be extinguished. God was touching the lives of the multitudes through missionaries, evangelists, and people who were just willing to pray.

I listened to the audio Bible as well, especially if I was sick in bed. During those times, I heard the gospel in a whole new way. It was alive, and it breathed life into every part of me. I had pressing questions about what certain scriptures meant, and I harassed and badgered anyone I considered a mature Christian in my hunger to understand more.

On this particular Sunday, the young pastor blustered his way through his answers after lunch. I'm sure he and his wife couldn't wait to leave our house, but this lady—me—who was clearly bonkers, was not going to give him a break for the afternoon.

When I could find no actual answers to my questions, I would sit in my room or lie on my bed and throw my questions out to God. Of course, we can look up anything on the internet, but it's nothing like getting our answers straight from the Holy Spirit. For me, the impact of bringing my questions to God directly was life changing and lasting.

～

One particular week, something had bothered me. I had read the passage in the Bible that describes Jesus walking to a place called Calvary, a hill outside of Jerusalem, where He would be crucified. Jesus had just been whipped with a *flagrum,* a short piece of braided leather tipped with lead. This had the effect of ripping the skin, sometimes down to the bone. After this, a crown of thorns was placed upon His head, bloodying His face, and no doubt dripping into His nose, eyes and mouth.

In His severely weakened state, carrying a cross would have been difficult for Jesus, if not almost impossible. It was at this point the Bible says,

> *Now as they led Him away, they laid hold of a certain man, Simon a Cyrenian, who was coming from the country, and on*

SIMON

him they laid the cross that he might bear it after Jesus.
Luke 23v26

Cyrene was a coastal town in modern-day Libya, in Africa. Since Simon came from this area of the world, he would most likely have been dark skinned, if not black. I am no biblical scholar, so I wasn't interested in a dissertation over his skin colour. I just came to the logical conclusion that this man would have some shade of darker skin.

By this time, however, I'd heard the Holy Spirit speak the words, "Nothing is coincidence," and as a result, I'd discovered that so much of what is written in the Bible has a deeper truth. As I lay in bed that night, I threw out my question to the Holy Spirit. "Lord," I said out loud, "why was Simon of Cyrene chosen to carry Jesus' cross, and why does it matter that he was a man of African descent?"

Once again it was as if my heart was being opened as God spoke to my spirit, bringing revelation and depth of understanding: *"Throughout history, indigenous and black people have often been forced to carry a heavy burden. But just as Simon of Cyrene carried my cross for me, I too will carry the indigenous and black person's cross throughout time, if they will let me."*

I lay in the dark and started to cry. Not only had I heard these words, I had felt the power behind them. In that moment I forcibly felt the grief of racism and discrimination. It was almost overwhelming to me. So much wrong had been done to so many people throughout history—slavery, dishonour, and stripping people of their land, denying so many the dignity all humans deserve—and all because of greed, self-righteousness, and hate. There were those who even believed their evil purpose was a call of God. But it never was God; it was people who used God's name to build upon a lie. Once again, I was aware that there was more to the picture than what Simon did for Jesus on the day of His crucifixion.

For a few days following, I wasn't well. I can't remember what caused me to be laid up in bed, but I recall that as I lay resting, two words were running on repeat through my mind, and I realised that the Holy Spirit was trying to tell me something. To me, the words sounded as if they were in the Māori language. Over and over, I kept hearing the words, "Te Rongopai, Te Rongopai." I decided that when I was better, I might go to the library to look for a Māori dictionary.

As soon as I was well again, I went back to work. My children were at primary school at the time, and I was working part-time in a Salvation Army thrift store. That day, I unlocked the shop, turned the lights on, and went behind the counter to get ready.

I looked up as an early customer came through the door carrying a box. She was an attractive, older Māori lady. Placing the box on the counter she said that she thought we could perhaps give away the books inside. Then she turned and left. She was out of the door before I had time to say a proper thank you.

When I opened the box, I literally stopped breathing for a moment. On the front of every book were the words written in large letters, *Te Rongopai*. I grabbed one of the books and quickly opened it. First in Māori, then in English, I read the following words: *Te Rongopai, The New Testament of the Bible in Māori*. On reading further I saw that the words *Te Rongopai* actually meant 'The Good News'. These were the very words I had been hearing for days!

First the revelation about Simon of Cyrene, and then this. I understood that God was trying to show me something so great I knew that I didn't humanly have the power to grasp the height, depth or width of it. It was God's great love for the Māori people. I'd always known this, but now it was in a spirit-to-spirit way, God's Spirit to mine. In a deeper, more profound way, I could see historical and present events in our nation through different eyes and with a different heart.

I never really understood why this revelation happened to me, except that I had asked a question and God had given me an answer much greater than I could ever have imagined.

May we never forget that God values everyone, and that there is no discrimination in God's eyes. We all carry within ourselves unknown or known discrimination toward people who are not the same as us. I pray that God would uproot every action or thought that is not based on love, that everyone everywhere would come to know the vastness of God's great love for them, regardless of where they come from or who they are.

- 14 -

A Miracle

The day seemed endless, and I couldn't wait to go home and hop into a bath. Sometimes this helped relieve the constant ache in my knees. I loved my job with the Open Home Foundation and enjoyed seeing the great outcomes in the lives of children who were placed in loving foster homes. But my days were now overshadowed by knee pain. It had grown worse over the previous few months to the point where I was finding it difficult to sit still in staff meetings or behind my desk.

I was quite young to have arthritis in my knees and didn't want to have knee replacements, so I was doing my best to live with the pain. Now this was becoming almost impossible. I would often sit through staff meetings trying not to cry with the level of pain I was experiencing.

My desk was opposite Sandra's. Sandra Perreaux managed the accounts, but I had first met her and her husband at church, where they worked as a team, ministering healing and deliverance to many.

I think it's important for those who spend their time reaching out to people in need, to balance that out with a good sense of humour and the ability to have fun. Well, Sandra has that ability in spades. Her personality almost jumps out of her eyes, which sparkle like diamonds when she laughs. She was a great friend at work, and lots of fun to be around.

Sandra had asked me to join her in attending a women's gathering in a building on the Wellington waterfront. On this particular evening there was to be a guest speaker from Australia, and it promised to be a good night out.

Sandra picked me up in her car and off we went. As usual, I was soon gasping for breath, as Sandra had the car heater cranked up so high that my clothes were sticking to my back. She had been used to a warmer climate further north before she moved to Wellington, and we laughed and joked about this as we made our way into town that night.

The air was buzzing with excitement. Sandra and I nabbed two great seats not far from the front. We had a good view of the proceedings, yet we were far enough back not to be noticed. I didn't recognise anyone and was wondering if this was going to be like a regular church service, or something different.

After the introduction we sang a few songs. It would have been enjoyable except that night my knees felt as though they were being hit with a jackhammer. Pain seared through me as I tried to stand and sing.

Finally, we were asked to sit. I hoped that taking the weight off my legs would lessen the pain—but it only got worse. I was no longer listening to what the lady at the front was saying. The throbbing in my knees distracted me so much I just wanted to go home.

Not wanting to ruin Sandra's night, I came up with a plan. I would tell her I was going to take a walk outside to hopefully lessen the pain in my knees, then I would wait in the foyer until the event came to a close. Feeling like a lone escapee taking off for the exit door, I was just about to make a dash for it, when the guest speaker started walking to the microphone. I realised that leaving at this point would cause a bit of a scene. Annoyed at myself for not taking my chance earlier when everyone was standing, I plonked myself down in my seat once more.

The speaker was introduced, then proceeded to tell us that while she was still in Australia making preparations for that night's service, the Holy Spirit had spoken to her. He told her that a woman would be present in the meeting who had arthritis in her knees and would be in a lot of pain. She was to make a call out to all the women present, and she would know the lady when she stepped out of her seat and came forward. She then called anyone who felt it could be them to come to the front.

Naturally there was a general rumble of ladies getting up and out of their seats, because arthritic knees are something many people suffer from. But I knew that the woman she was referring to was me.

As soon as I stood up, she pointed at me and asked me to move to the front. At this point I was so desperate I would have knocked down chairs just to get there. The speaker prayed a general prayer for the healing of arthritis for the others who had come forward, and then turned her attention to me.

I don't know what I expected at that moment. Maybe I thought I would feel heat shooting through my knees or possibly sense something spiritual, but nothing happened. Nothing that I was aware of, anyway. I'm always available for something grand, such as an angel flying past in a gold chariot, but it wasn't to be. I felt nothing and I saw nothing. But I had an assurance that the Holy Spirit had spoken to her in Australia about me, so I believed it was done. I never went for a walk around the building that night but stayed for the rest of the service, and the pain was definitely more tolerable.

The following morning, I took care of my family, then went to work. I was immediately aware that the pain had lessened but was still there—not as a blinding pain, but still an irritating type of pain. I was rather disappointed, as I had been looking forward to having my first day in a long time when my knees didn't hurt. I guess I was also hoping to share with everyone at work the wonderful healing I'd received the night before.

Sitting behind my desk I could feel the jackhammer starting up again. *What was I to do? What was I to do?* Then I thought of something. The Bible is full of promises of healing. I would write down a few of them, and every time the pain started I would repeat one of those scriptures:

> *Beloved, I pray that you may prosper in all things and be in health, just as your soul prospers.*
> *3 John 2*

A MIRACLE

"For I will restore health to you and heal you of your wounds," says the Lord.
Jeremiah 13v17

Your words have upheld him who was stumbling, and you have strengthened the feeble knees.
Job 4v4

There were so many promises of healing in the Bible, but I knew I could only choose a few at a time or I would be reading them out loud all day.

Soon I had my list ready to go. I decided if I felt the pain, I would speak out a verse about healing. Some of them may have been slightly out of context, but I figured it didn't matter. God knew what I was on about.

The next time pain hit my knees I hid my mouth behind my hands, because I was at work, and read out loud a healing scripture. Then I did it again. To my surprise the pain seemed to ebb away!

Well, I didn't need encouragement after that. The pain seemed to lessen a lot, and now I was off—in the car, at home, at the washing line, at my desk... you name it, if a pain hit, I said a healing scripture! I must have looked like I had been on the drink and was talking to an invisible friend, but I didn't care. In some respects, I guess I was! I was talking to God and holding up His promises before Him.

At first, I seemed to be saying them all day. But then something wonderful started to happen. The pain in my knees began to disappear. I noticed that whereas I had been repeating the scriptures all day, it was now only hourly. In no time at all, it was only once a day. Within six weeks there was no need for me to repeat them at all! The pain was gone. From that day until this, the pain in my knees has never bothered me again.

Time marched on. Many years later, we were living on a large section with beautiful trees scattered about the edges and at intermittent places on the expansive lawn. They had clearly seen many seasons and had lived long enough to see people come and go and enjoy living in the house that was now ours. But there was one thing that was a real chore about these trees. During autumn, they would lose their leaves.

The ground was covered in leaves. To me, a lovely vista had changed into a sea of brown and red. They covered everything from the lawn and the concrete to our carpet if they got inside. So, I swept them and I swept them and I swept them. I should have given up, but it became a battle between me and the leaves. Soon it became apparent that the leaves were winning.

One day I felt a nasty twang in my right knee. Ignoring it, I carried on sweeping. The next morning, I awoke to find a large grapefruit in my bed. On closer inspection it wasn't a grapefruit at all, it was my knee! It was a monster. I soon realised it wasn't going to go away overnight, and took myself off to an orthopaedic specialist.

Sitting in the consultation room, I awaited the diagnosis. I had a torn meniscus. In time it should heal and I needed to elevate my leg when possible. But it was what the specialist told me next that really threw me. He said he could see evidence of arthritis in both my knees, and was happy to do knee replacements if I felt I needed them. It was over twenty years since I'd even had a twinge in my knees, and now he was telling me this!

I sat back and looked at this man with the most incredulous expression on my face. Without thinking, I told him not to be so ridiculous and that I didn't have arthritis in my knees. I must have sounded like an unstable person who was living in denial. But I was just so shocked. *No pain, no symptoms all these years, and he tells me this!*

He was so surprised at my reaction that he burst out laughing. I mean, it was almost a leg-slapping, throw your head back kind of laugh. I don't think he had ever encountered this sort of reaction before. Then I started laughing too. I saw the funny side of my reaction and we parted that day still chuckling at my refusal to accept what he had told me.

That afternoon I paced around my kitchen. *How could he tell me he saw arthritis, and yet I had no symptoms, ever?* That sent me on a trail. Are there different types of miracles? After prayer and consulting trusted friends and looking in the Bible, I soon discovered there are.

Firstly, there is the creative miracle. That is when someone receives a new body part, or a tumour vanishes leaving the person as if the condition had never afflicted them at all. Then there is the type of miracle that stops disease in its tracks—this is what I believe happened to my knees. There was evidence of historical disease but it had never developed any further and I had no symptoms at all. I also believe a surgeon can perform miraculous healing through surgery. God uses all three and possibly even more, such as medication.

Once I began to understand that I couldn't box God in and expect Him to work according to a set formula, I felt released. I needed to understand why the specialist saw what he did even though I knew by the evidence in my life that I had received healing.

Time has moved on, and my knees continue to perform as they should. I walk long distances and enjoy the fact that I live without pain in my knees. I am thankful Sandra took me to that women's meeting that day. I look forward to many more years of using my now older, bonier, and wrinklier knees.

If you need a miracle in your life, don't feel that one size fits all. God will work in a way that He knows is right for you. God will not be hemmed in by our limited thinking. Just enjoy the fact that He knows your situation, and that your particular healing, when it comes, is tailor made just for you.

- 15 -

The Bible Tells Me So

I can still hear the sound of children's voices around me as I sang this song in Sunday School with my friends. It is one that has been sung around the world, in many languages, by both adults and children alike.

Jesus loves me, this I know,
For the Bible tells me so.
Little ones to Him belong,
They are weak but He is strong.

Yes, Jesus loves me,
Yes, Jesus loves me,
Yes, Jesus loves me,
The Bible tells me so.

Much of the Bible's message is simple and not meant to be difficult to understand.

I remember reading a book about a man who came into a relationship with God, and during a time of healing he began to understand what the Bible said about the devil and the occult. As he recounted his past experiences, he explained that just as the Bible tells us simply that God loves us, it also says in simple words that we should stay far away from the occult in all its forms. He wrote that dabbling with such things is dangerous and will ultimately have negative consequences in our lives, and that the devil (also known as Satan) is the great counterfeiter of all things good, yet his ultimate aim is our destruction.

So, I was reading this book and learning much. At this time in my life I had not long given my life back over to God, and I was going through a period of inner healing. My self-esteem and belief that I knew anything much of value was still low, and I looked up to men and women I saw as mature Christians.

Around this time we were on holiday as a family, taking a tour of the South Island of New Zealand. An elderly couple we knew through mutual friends, who had worked as missionaries in Africa, had asked that we visit them while we were in the South Island. This couple were now retired and living in New Zealand. We decided it would be nice to stop in and see them.

Driving up a long winding driveway, we saw two houses that had been built on the land. One was new and small and had been built for the elderly, retired missionaries, and the other house belonged to their son. The second house was large, and a beautiful statement of architecture from days gone by. Looking around, it appeared to me that this was a small piece of paradise on which these parents could enjoy their final years.

I noticed quite a number of cars parked in front of the larger house and didn't think too much of it as we were primarily there to visit the parents who were waiting for us in the smaller house. I was rather excited to meet this man and his wife. He was a trained cleric from one of the more traditional denominations, and apparently was a recognised biblical scholar.

The moment I saw him I was even more impressed. He resembled a sage with his white hair and long white beard. His face wore the lines of a man who appeared to have studied long into the night, with the only light available being that of a small, flickering candle. Just being around this man made me nervous, and I waited for him to take his seat before I took mine. For some reason it was just me and this man in the lounge for about ten minutes. I think Geoff may have gone to help the elderly lady in the kitchen while she prepared us some afternoon tea.

The many questions that had previously been whirring around in my head seemed to be now stuck in my throat, and I sat in complete silence. Then the Reverend (that's what I called him) spoke. He asked if I was reading any good books, and if so what were they about?

Now here was my moment. I was sure he would be most impressed that I was reading a book about a man's journey towards inner healing and what the Bible teaches about the occult. I told the Reverend about the book and waited for his acknowledgement and approval.

He looked at me, squinted his eyes and to my surprise said, "Well, I wouldn't know about such things. We don't believe there is such a thing as evil. When the Bible talks about evil being in the world, it really just means we are fighting our inner selves. You should meet our visitor from Africa. He is staying in the other house with my son and daughter-in-law. He believes he is called by God to help educate people and set them free from evil. But for me, I don't believe there is a devil at all."

At that moment, it was as if two worlds were colliding. I had seen the power of darkness and its effects. I had evidenced the wickedness in this world, and yet here was a man of God telling me it was all baloney! It took me by such surprise that I started to shake. *You mean all I have learned in the Bible has some sort of deceptive, paradoxical meaning? It doesn't mean what it says? How had I missed that?* Here was a man that in my sight was studied and great, and I on the other hand, had read only parts of the Bible and a few books. I was nobody, he was somebody.

I was stunned. My head was swimming. I didn't even challenge him. I just accepted he knew more than me, even though what he said made no sense at all.

I am disappointed to admit I was so easily taken in by someone just because they had a title and looked like a learned person. I took myself off to the toilet. All I could think to do was to get alone somewhere and pray. I wanted at that moment to be on my own with God, even if it meant it was in someone's toilet.

It was rather a bonus to discover this toilet actually had carpet on the floor, so I decided to get on my knees and pray. So there I was in this couple's home, hiding in the toilet on my knees and praying.

I remember asking God to please somehow get the young man from Africa to speak to me—a big ask, considering we were not even in the same house. I asked God to show me if all that I had experienced and read about in the Bible warning us of the existence of the devil was real, and to somehow get this man from Africa to tell me. I hadn't even seen him or met him yet, but that's what I asked for that day.

I came back into the lounge room to find Geoff and the other couple getting ready to leave. It had been decided, in my absence, that we would all go over to the big house to say hello to the son and daughter-in-law. Off we went, up the path and into the kitchen, through a back door.

This house was majestic. It oozed character and charm, and I loved it from the moment I stepped inside. Through the kitchen, I could see into a large lounge room. It was full of people standing around talking, and they seemed to be gravitating towards someone in the corner. Moving towards the doorway, I could see it was the gentleman from Africa, who appeared to be saying his goodbyes.

I found myself alone in the kitchen with the son, still upset by the events in the smaller house. I felt as if all I believed in had been thrown into question. Because of this, I suppose I may have appeared a little rude. Without niceties, I jumped in and asked whether he believed in the existence of evil in this world? Knowing that he was heavily involved in his local church, I assumed he believed what the Bible said about such things. He answered quite casually, as if it was just a big nothing to him. Little did he know how much it meant to me. "Oh, no," he replied, "We are just fighting our inner man. There is no such thing as evil."

There it was, that same sentence once again. Not knowing what to say, I went into the lounge room and made my way to the back so as not to disturb the twenty or so guests. I hadn't met any of these people and felt particularly unseen by anyone in the room, including the departing visitor from Africa.

It was at this point that the man from Africa stopped talking to his guests and started scanning the room. As soon as his eyes fell on me, he paused, and then loud and clear he spoke the following words: "Sister, you and I will never meet again on this side of heaven. But the love you have for God shines upon your face. The Lord wants you to know something, and it is that *He who is in you is greater than he who is in the world.*"

Everyone was taken by surprise. They hadn't seen me before, and there appeared no reason for him to speak to me. They looked at me, confused. *What made him say that?* I turned and saw the man who had just told me he didn't believe there was evil in the world, and his mouth had dropped open. He knew what those words meant.

I knew what those words meant too. They were taken from the Bible:

You are of God, little children, and have overcome them, because He who is in you is greater than he who is in the world.
1 John 4v4

'He who is in the world' refers to the devil and the evil power he exerts in this world, and 'He who is in me' refers to God living in me through His Holy Spirit. This man had not only answered my question, he had used a Bible verse to do it! God had answered my prayer! This man had just verified to me that evil exists, but that God living within and through His people is far greater than any evil in this world.

I saw that the greatest ruse of the devil was to get people, especially Christians, to believe that he didn't exist at all!

As everyone started chatting again, I slipped out of the lounge room and into an empty hallway. Quietly I whispered to God, "Thank you."

God doesn't care if a person is highly educated or illiterate. He doesn't care if we are old or young, or what we look like or what we wear. He is interested in our hearts—that's what matters to Him.

The years have gone by and I have grown stronger. I have also come to understand that not everybody who has the appearance of great knowledge or understanding, or even acts as if they are spiritual, are really what they portray themselves to be. Don't follow every storyline you hear and believe it to be true. Ask God to show you the truth, and read the Bible, even if it is only a few verses a day.

All these years later I still believe there is one thing I know to be true, and I know it for sure:

Yes, Jesus loves me,
Yes, Jesus loves me,
Yes, Jesus loves me,
The Bible tells me so.

- 16 -

Te Mona

It was my birthday, and I was looking forward to some retail therapy with my niece, Melinda. Melinda would have been in her late teens at the time, and it was very charitable of her to give up her morning to hang out with her aunt. I had decided I wanted to buy a special ring for myself. We were going to a jewellery shop to hopefully choose something lovely.

I had withdrawn cash from the bank and put it in a small plastic bag. Why I did this I have no idea. It was likely that I thought that if I had only a certain amount of cash on hand rather than a credit card, I wouldn't blow the budget. It was quite a substantial amount of money for us at the time, and I felt I was being rather extravagant.

We arrived at the shopping mall and had morning tea. Melinda was good company, and her happy laughter brought a sense of fun to the occasion. We sauntered around the mall looking through stores and eventually headed to Kmart. From there we would go to the jewellery shop where I would hopefully make my birthday purchase.

But then a strange thing started to happen. It came on me slowly and settled somewhere in my heart. What had sounded like a wonderful idea ten minutes ago had now begun to feel less and less exciting. I pushed the feeling away. I was looking forward to a fancy ring, and after all, it was my birthday. I loved the feeling of anticipation and was rather disappointed that this emotion was now disappearing. Instead, I was feeling decidedly flat. In fact, as we made our way around the store, I realised I really didn't want a ring at all.

I didn't want Melinda to feel I had dragged her to the shops on false pretences, so I said nothing as we cruised around the aisles looking at all the items on display. Then an idea started to form in my mind. I had noticed a Kmart employee at the entrance of the shop, but had not really paid much attention to him. He just stood there, nodding and smiling at everyone as they came in and out of the store. He also checked receipts to ensure people did not leave with items they had not paid for.

I decided I was going to give him the money I had set aside to purchase a ring. I don't know where the idea came from. It was suddenly there, and I knew that's what I wanted to do with it. I would give the man at the entrance to Kmart the money that was meant for my birthday.

The moment I had this idea, the flat feeling I had about buying myself a ring, lifted. It was like a weight was taken off my heart. I now had no desire to own a silly ring, and I couldn't wait to give the money away. I was rather nervous that the man might be insulted or think I had lost my mind, but that was a risk I was willing to take. My first hurdle was to tell Melinda.

Looking at my niece, I told her I didn't want a ring and I was going to give the money to the man who worked at the entrance of Kmart. She looked at me and put her hand to her mouth in shock. Now, she was used to my crazy behaviour, but this time I'm sure she thought I'd truly lost the plot. All she could say was, "Tante Janet!"—*tante* being Dutch for 'aunt'. I could tell she thought I'd taken leave of my senses. But now I was on a mission, and nothing was going to stop me.

We made our way to where the man was standing. As usual, he was nodding and smiling at all the customers as they came and went. Soon we were close enough to enact my plan. Moving quickly before I had time to stop myself, I almost ran up to him. Without much thought I said, "Excuse me, but I believe God has told me to give you this money today."

I shoved the plastic bag towards him. I think I stuck it in his shirt pocket, but maybe I put it in his hand. It was all a bit of a blur because I was embarrassed, and I wanted to make a run for it. Melinda and I got away as fast as we could walk, but as I got about fifteen feet away, I turned back to see his reaction.

The man was still standing in the same spot, staring our way. He looked like he was starting to cry. My mind began to race. *Had I hurt his feelings? Was he embarrassed? Had I done the wrong thing?* I didn't know, but I kept going, and Melinda and I went home.

About a week later, I returned to the mall with my father. At this point in his life, he was elderly and could no longer drive, so from time to time I took him to a café in the mall, just outside the entrance to Kmart.

As we sat enjoying our coffee that day, I turned to see the man who had been on the door the week before. He was signalling to me, so I told Dad I would be back in a minute and went over to talk to him.

It was the first time I had paid much attention to this man. He was always doing his job, smiling and nodding—I guess he was almost so familiar that I didn't really notice him anymore. Little did I know that I was about to meet someone very important.

Introducing himself, he told me his name was Te Mona. I could tell he was of Māori or Pacific Island descent. His face was kind, and he wore his longish hair tied back. Te Mona then told me what had happened the day I gave him the money.

The week earlier, he said, he had been sick and had taken some time off to recuperate. When his next pay cheque arrived, however, there was a mistake. He hadn't been paid the sick leave owing to him. The problem was being sorted out, but meanwhile he had been left short and didn't have enough money to pay for his food or bills.

Te Mona then told me that he was a Christian. While he was standing at work doing his job, he had been quietly praying. Now for those who feel God needs to hear perfect pious and beautiful prayers from us, I would like to educate you. God loves it when we are real. He wants to hear if we are sad, hurt or unhappy, or happy and content. He wants us to be real. God is not interested in fakeness, just reality and truth from the heart.

That day, Te Mona was inwardly crying out to God. He told God that he didn't even have money to take care of himself let alone give to his church. He then asked God to prove to him that He was taking care of his financial needs.

It was at that very moment that I stepped up and gave Te Mona the money.

I felt excited to be part of his answer to prayer. I also felt humbled as I came to understand who this man was. Te Mona shared with me that when he said hello to people as they came and went from the store, he would pray for them. I was shocked. I mean, there were hundreds, if not thousands, of people coming in and out of that shop each week!

Looking at Te Mona as he spoke, I realised I was standing in the presence of someone rather special—a man of honour, integrity and faith; a man most people ignored because he was always there, just doing the same thing.

Little did they realise they were walking past a king—not a perfect man, as I am sure he would readily admit, but a king in God's eyes, nonetheless. People who otherwise might never have been lifted up in prayer to God, would be if they walked past Te Mona at work.

I thank God I met Te Mona and had the privilege to be part of something bigger than myself. Te Mona at this point in time still stands at the entrance of Kmart and blesses people with his friendly and welcoming smile. I still like nice rings, but I couldn't care less if I owned them or not. At the end of the day, they're all just trinkets, and we will leave them behind. But Te Mona is building riches that will never pass away, and that is so much bigger and lasting than anything worldly wealth can bring.

Thank you, Te Mona, for all the lives you touch. Thank you for all the prayers you pray, and for your kind smile that greets so many people as they go about their business each day.

- 17 -

Friendship

I've already introduced you to my friends Mel and Janet. Together we are like a threefold cord. They have brought strength, joy and correction into my life. There are other women I also consider friends, and I am so thankful for each of them. My adult daughter Kimberley is one of them. She loves me too much to spare my feelings at times and will bring me truth when I need to hear it. But there is another person who has been with me at the coalface of life.

I met Viv through mutual friends when my children were around eight and ten. The moment I met her I was struck by how beautiful she was. She had porcelain skin accentuated by jet black hair that was short and layered and seemed to naturally stick out in all the right places. I thought she looked like someone who could have graced the cover of Vogue. She too was a Christian, and although I didn't know it at the time, she had walked through the deepest of valleys and found her faith when she was in the darkest of places.

As soon as I met Vivienne, I liked her a lot. Something inside me recognised that she had a depth to her, and I wanted to know more about her story. I remember that feeling, and I remember telling myself that I didn't even know her and that to bluntly ask her to meet me for coffee might come across as a bit weird. So, I left it at that and went on my way and didn't see her again for a long time.

It must have been about two years later that I was heading out to the local shopping mall. As I was walking to my garage, a picture flashed through my mind of this woman I had met two years earlier. In the picture, she was wearing a light green shirt and a tailored jacket. I could even see the colour of her trousers. It didn't even occur to me that I was having a 'God-moment', so I just discarded the thought and went out the door, got into my car, and set off to the mall.

Walking through the mall, I made my way to the pharmacy. Opposite the pharmacy was a trendy clothing shop. I looked over towards the clothes shop to admire the fashionable clothes on display in the shop window. Then I stopped to take a second look, because there, standing outside the shop, leaning against the window, was the very lady I had met a couple of years before, wearing the exact outfit I had seen in my mind when I left my house fifteen minutes ago!

At that moment I got so excited that I'd clearly had some sort of mini vision that I ran towards her and started talking excitedly. I asked her if she remembered me, and told her that I had seen an image of her in my mind's eye just before I left home and that she was wearing exactly the same clothes as I'd seen in that image!

To my relief, she was kind enough not to start running away from me, and we began to chat. Viv said she had been living in England for the past year with her husband and three children and had not long arrived back in New Zealand. We arranged to meet, and I looked forward to hearing more about her overseas trip and her life.

But it wasn't going to be a one-off cup of coffee and a chat. It was going to become a relationship that would change and enrich my life. She and I, along with Janet and Mel, would walk together, each bringing our own gifting and strength to our relationships with one another. I suppose in that respect, we were to become a fourfold cord, and although we are now living in different places and living different lives, our relationships continue to this day.

In Viv I soon discovered a woman who loved God above all else. She was like a firebrand in her faith and stood up without fear for what she considered to be right. We were both learning and growing and going through inner healing at the time. I guess, in truth, we were unrefined. We saw things in black and white, and sometimes we didn't see them from the same vantage point. Although I laugh about it now, we disagreed on some issues quite strongly, both feeling like we were in the right and the other had got it wrong. The passing of time has mellowed us both, and God has used our relationship over the years like sandpaper to refine our rougher edges.

We all need someone willing to tell us the truth rather than agree with everything we say just to keep the peace and pander to us. Today Viv is an editor for a popular and well-read Christian magazine, and her strength in speaking the truth is something God is using powerfully to touch many people's lives throughout our nation.

I recall being sick for about three months, really sick. I had repeated kidney infections, and the cause could not be found. I lay on the couch day after day so exhausted I could barely function. My back would burn around the location of my kidneys, and I would ache and feel miserable. The doctor prescribed antibiotics again and again, which helped to a point. I didn't leave home except to visit the emergency department when the flare-ups got bad. All I could think to do was to flush my kidneys with copious amounts of water from our water-filter tap.

My friends knew about my situation. *How could they not?* I whinged day and night. I would call to ask for prayer, and moan and groan. In truth, I was the friend of your nightmares.

One day I rang Viv, yet again, to ask her to pray for me. This time I asked her to ask the Holy Spirit to speak to her and tell her why I was so sick. Each time I asked for prayer it would be for healing, but this time I wanted to know the cause of the affliction. Now God could have revealed the cause of the problem to me personally, but He didn't. I think this is because it is important that we are connected to other people and don't become too self-reliant. At the end of the day, it's not healthy for us to become too independent as this can set us on the wrong path and cause us to make poor decisions. All of us have the potential to become 'that person' who, without the check and balance of another, can go astray in some area of our life.

So, we prayed and waited. Nothing. I could hear her breathing on the other end of the phone. Then, out of the blue, Viv asked me if I had a water-filter tap. I told her proudly that I was using it all day, every day, to hydrate and flush out my kidneys. Then she asked me, "Have you ever had the filter changed? I strongly feel it's something to do with your water filter!"

Pardon? I had never used a water filter before living in this house. What did she mean by having the filter changed? This may sound so dim to anyone who knows about these things, but how do you know if no one tells you?

I ran to the sink, opened the cupboard below, and there it was, a filter. With the phone in one hand and grasping the filter with the other, I removed the filter from the attachment to the tap and opened it up.

It was full of gunge! It was gross. We had purchased this house from an elderly couple who obviously had no idea about water filters either. Who knew you were meant to replace the filter every six months, and at the most, a year?!

I had been poisoning myself! In an effort to help myself, I had been using the filter tap even more than usual. Because I was too sick to leave the house, I was drinking from it twenty-four hours a day!

Viv had listened to the Holy Spirit and was willing to share something that sounded so out of left field that it hardly seemed likely. But she had heard right. That was the last time I drank from that tap until the filter was changed. After three months of agony, I was totally restored in three days. By the grace of God my kidneys didn't sustain any permanent damage. I am now hyper-vigilant with changing the tap filter, as well as the water filter attached to the chiller on my fridge.

I look back at the issue with the water filter as an analogy about friends. Friends and family can act like filters. Some relationships are unhealthy—they can be too familiar, or co-dependent. If we get too close to people who are not good for us, the result can be like drinking from a filthy, germ-infested water filter. It will poison us in the end. A healthy friendship, on the other hand, is a great blessing—something to be treasured and nurtured and cared for.

But what is friendship? Friendship doesn't necessarily mean finding someone just like ourselves. Friendships can be with a spouse, a parent, or someone who just wants to share part of their life with you. Each friendship will have its own qualities and value and reason for being in your life. A friend is someone who has your back and is willing to bring correction if they feel something is bad for you. A true friend will always have your best interests at heart.

In a world where independence is highly valued, we can sometimes forget that we actually need other people. God does not want us to be lone rangers in this world. We have to learn to think for ourselves, but it's not healthy to be so isolated that we have no one to share our thoughts and experiences with. In the words of Ecclesiastes 4:9-12:

> *Two are better than one because they have a good reward for their labor. For if they fall, one will lift up his companion. But woe to him who is alone when he falls, for he has no one to help him up. Again, if two lie down together, they will keep warm; but how can one be warm alone? Though one may be overpowered by another, two can withstand him. And a threefold cord is not quickly broken.*

You may just have one person who is there for you, or you may have more, but treasure them and listen to them and be willing to take respectful correction. It may be a relative, it may be a friend but give them permission to speak into your life, if you need it, and you into theirs.

You may be in a season where you feel you have no true friend to turn to. That's okay. Talking to God like a friend is a relationship too. Even a dog or a cat can be a friend in their own special way. Relationships are important, sometimes painful, and often wonderful. Treasure each other and don't try and go it alone because someone out there just might need you as a friend today.

- 18 -

A Glimpse

When my children were young it was a season of brilliant sunshine. I enjoyed being a mother and all that encompassed. But it was also a season of dark, stormy rain-clouds. At times I was so unwell that family members would have to take care of my children. During the dark times, books became a lifeline to my faith.

I sometimes enjoyed the luxury of having a long bath when the children were at school or otherwise occupied with Geoff, and I would always take a good book with me. I'd hardly notice that the once-warm blanket of bath water had turned cold, because I was so engrossed by what I was reading.

One day I was lost in the true adventures of a lady who had survived being imprisoned in a prisoner of war camp during World War II. She told of miracles and God-moments all wrapped up within the horrors of death and war, and how the light of God in the prison camp was brighter than any evil rendered upon her by the Nazi guards in that awful place. She inspired me and taught me a lot about getting through the valleys of life.

At one point in the book the author wrote how she had experienced, 'a glimpse of God's glory'. I thought this sounded pretty fantastic, and because I wanted more of God's presence in my life, I threw out a request. From the comfort of my bath, I asked God for a glimpse of His glory. What that meant, I wasn't too sure, but it sounded good to me. Pulling the plug on the now lukewarm water, I got out of the bath and continued with my day.

That night, I lay awake in bed. Geoff was asleep, and I was unaware of anything except the sound of his breathing and the noise of the wind outside. I felt nothing unusual and sensed nothing different. Then, without prelude, something began to appear in my vision. I was wide awake, so it wasn't a dream, and it was as clear and real as everything else around me. I was lying on my back looking towards the ceiling when it began. Strange as it seems, I felt no fear, nor did it occur to me that something highly unusual was happening.

I saw what appeared to be a largish window, perhaps five feet high and six feet wide, coming down towards me. As it moved closer, I saw what looked like a woody climbing plant, the sort that winds its way around a trellis, only in this case it was wrapped around the entire window frame. Once it came close enough, I noticed it was thorny and had no leaves. I recognised it was exactly like the crown of thorns that was placed upon the head of Jesus before His crucifixion, except that in my vision it was entwined around the window frame.

It all felt so normal as I lay there taking it all in. Then without warning, I felt myself lift out of my bed and rise up through that window frame. Now, in reality, I don't think that my body left the bed at all, but either I was having a vision that was extremely real or my spirit was being taken by God and was not with my body in that moment in time. I do not know and I cannot explain it. If I did, I would no doubt have to try and work it out theologically, and that's not what it was about for me. I just knew what was happening was real; I was not asleep and having a dream.

I thought a lot about sharing what happened next. Language has too many limitations to adequately express what I experienced that night. All I can say is, I found myself in another place. I was in a meadow, standing in a field of about five-inch-long grass. In front of me was a tree, and in the distance, I could see more trees. I saw and heard no one.

I looked around, amazed. It was as if I had new vision. I felt like one of those people you see in videos who is colour blind but is handed EnChroma glasses and is able to see the full spectrum of colours for the very first time. Magnify that by a thousand and you might have an idea of the colours I was seeing. Greens were far greener, blues were much bluer, and so on. The spectrum of colours was so much greater than I had known, as if every shade of colour had life within it.

The trees were majestic, stunning and glorious. I could hear birds singing, and the sound of it made the most beautiful bird-calls on earth sound dull in comparison. It was as if the finger of God was in all the nature surrounding me. Everything was alive!

But nothing in this spectacular vista compared to what I sensed. I've heard evil described as a sense of 'heaviness', but I never realised how much it weighs on us here in the world. With a complete absence of evil, it was as if a ton of rocks had been lifted off my back. The sense of unabandoned love and joy was without the filter of darkness, and it had no end.

God's presence was everywhere. I felt His acceptance and love, and I did not want to leave this place, ever. Time had no meaning; my life on earth meant nothing. I felt as if I was finally home. I didn't just want to stay and enjoy the experience, it was way more than that. This was where I belonged. I never, ever wanted to go back.

The moment I had this thought, I felt a pull.

The next thing I was aware of was that I was moving backwards, back through the window frame that was surrounded by the thorny plant, and then I was back in my bed. I quickly turned to look at Geoff. He was still fast asleep. I looked up, but the window frame was gone. All I could see was the outline of my bedroom furniture in the dark.

My mind started to race. *What had just happened to me?*

"What was that?" I blurted out.

Immediately I heard a response. It was the clear, concise, and beautiful voice of the Holy Spirit. He said, "You asked for a glimpse of My glory."

Then I remembered the bath, and my request. Never had I imagined the answer would come in this way. I don't know what I expected, but it wasn't this. My mind started to go over everything that had just happened.

A crown of thorns. Thorns wrapped around the window frame. A scripture went through my mind:

> *And the soldiers twisted a crown of thorns*
> *and put it on His head.*
> *John 19v2*

I thought of how Jesus paved the way for us to be in heaven for eternity. 1 Corinthians 2:9 says, "Eye has not seen, nor ear heard, nor has it entered into the heart of man the things that God has prepared for those who love Him."

I lay there for some time going over what had happened again and again. I knew in my heart that if faced with a choice of coming back to my life on earth, I would have said no. I would love to have been a bit more heroic and recognised that my life here still had a purpose and that my family needed me, but I wasn't. I had received a glimpse of what God had prepared, and that was more than enough. I wanted to be back there and not here. I believe that's why my experience was so short. The pull to stay was too great.

Our life in this world is not a beginning and an end, it's just the beginning. I glimpsed the smallest of fragments, but it was more than enough. It changed me and the way I look at life. I try not to sweat the small stuff. I see skirmishes and the things people get upset about, and I want to say, just let it go. There is so much for us to do while we are here, and we mustn't get side-tracked with irrelevant stuff.

I am mindful that we are here on this earth for a reason and that to seek after constant spiritual experiences and supernatural encounters is not what it is all about. Loving God is what it is all about and that is what is important. Love others, look after others, and just know that while you are here there is still work for you to do. Don't sweat the small stuff; it can distract you from all you are called to do and be.

Wonderful things lie ahead for us in heaven, but meanwhile, live your life. Don't be so spiritually minded and focused on heaven that

A GLIMPSE

you are of no use to anyone here on earth. You have only got one shot at life, so grab it with both hands and live it with no regrets.

- 19 -

These Boots are Made for Walking

One day at work, I tripped over a heater and suffered a painful foot injury. My right ankle became swollen, and soon I could barely stand on that foot. I went to see the doctor, who quickly diagnosed a sprained ankle and sent me on my way. I was happy with that and looked forward to a quick recovery.

However, the injury persisted for many months. I was in constant pain. I would wince every time I used my right leg and was finding it difficult to work. Later that year I resigned from my job, hoping my foot would improve.

But this wasn't to be. Months went by, and still my ankle was painful, often to the point where the pain literally brought tears to my eyes. I took anti-inflammatories, which gave some short-term relief, and battled on. I wore boots that firmly supported my ankle everywhere I went. I sometimes thought that the boots made me look as if I was about to go and ride a horse, but I didn't care. They acted as a sort of splint and helped me get around. For a period, I managed to get hold of some crutches, but this caused pain in my shoulders and gave me headaches, so I gave up on the crutches.

My foot was now starting to look rather deformed and a little claw-like, and there was no noticeable improvement. Day after day I walked around cringing with the pain, hoping that sometime soon it would get better.

During this time, I was fixated on a popular song sung by a group called *Mary Mary*. It included the words, "Take the shackles off my feet so I can dance." I listened to it and sang it day and night as a sort of prayer to God to heal my foot.

I believe the song was meant to be sung with a happy-clappy attitude. But by this time, I was singing it with clenched teeth and a pinched expression as I dragged my foot around the place like it was caught in a large, invisible mouse-trap. I can imagine there were times I was not great company as I winced my way through life.

One afternoon I was at my sister Anne's house, and I noticed her Promise Box sitting on a coffee table. A Promise Box is a small container filled with separate bits of cardboard, and on each piece of cardboard is a promise from the Bible.

I loved Anne's Promise Box. I had seen plenty of these around, but none of them were like the one Anne owned. It was a lovely looking container with all the typewritten cards sticking out of the top.

On this particular day I was whining about my foot again when I spotted her box. Picking it up I asked God, yet again, to heal my foot. I then pulled out a card and read it. To my utmost surprise it read,

My eyes are ever toward the Lord, for He shall pluck my feet out of the net.
Psalm 25v15

What?! I read it again and got excited. Suddenly I had hope that my foot was going to be healed!

The healing began when Geoff decided one day that he'd had enough, and dragged me off to another doctor, demanding something be done. The doctor immediately referred me to a surgeon, and within a short space of time, an operation was scheduled. For some reason, I had pushed the injured foot problem to the bottom of the pile until it became an insurmountable issue that I didn't have the strength to face. I needed someone to step up for me, and I am thankful that Geoff did.

After the surgery I was allocated a zippy little wheelchair, and my family and I became adept at manoeuvring me around everywhere. For six weeks I lived in this chair, and for me it was a small window into another world.

I discovered that shop access can be appalling. I often found that I couldn't get around racks and signs because not enough room had been left for people in wheelchairs. I learned that able-bodied people would often hog wheelchair-access toilets. I would almost have an accident because I was stuck waiting for someone to finish their business while I sat in some drafty corridor outside.

I soon realised I was now part of a new gang. It was the wheelchair gang. It was like a world within a world that I hadn't been aware existed before. At the shopping mall, I noticed that others who were in wheelchairs chose to go there to shop and have coffee because the mall was undercover and easy to get around.

As I wheeled past another regular in a wheelchair there would be a sort of code. It consisted of looking at each other, raising our eyebrows and saying, "Hey" or "How's it going?" There was one gentleman who always high-fived me as he went past. I felt privileged to be part of this gang and enjoyed the unspoken camaraderie.

Some days I was glad I had the wheelchair to sit in because I would have been laughing so hard that if I had been standing, I don't think my legs could have supported me. Whoever was pushing me, often my daughter Kimberley, would be buckled up next to me holding onto the wheelchair to support themselves from falling over with laughter.

On one occasion we were in a shop that had the most enormous Christmas tree. It was covered in brightly coloured baubles, and it nearly touched the ceiling. As Kimberley was wheeling me past this tree, the arm of my wheelchair somehow snagged one of the branches. Unaware of the situation that was unfolding Kimberley kept moving at speed.

What happened then was rather like a slow-motion movie. I heard a sort of creak and then, out of the corner of my eye, I spotted a flash of bright colours. The entire tree was coming with us! With a mighty crash this great baubled mass fell to the ground, except for the part that was still attached to my chair.

At that moment I turned and saw the look of shock and horror on the shop manager's face. She looked as if she was going to plunge a knife into the heart of the terrible person who had dared to take her tree down. When she saw it was me, her face instantly changed to an expression that read, "Oh dear, it's a poor invalid who has knocked my tree down and just about destroyed my shop." You can imagine my relief. There had to be an upside to being in a wheelchair, and I guess this was it. We exited the shop as fast as we could without appearing like we were trying to escape the scene of a crime.

Another day I was enjoying an outing with my aunt who was visiting us from Holland. She was in her seventies, spritely and short in stature. She had been pushing me around in my wheelchair at the local shopping mall. We made it onto the escalator which carried us down to the floor below. At the bottom of the escalator there was a café in an open area of the mall, and nearby a large support pillar that went from the floor to the ceiling.

My aunt was standing in front of my wheelchair as we descended. As we neared the bottom of the escalator, my wheelchair got stuck. This was a recipe for disaster. I was trapped at the bottom of the escalator, while the escalator floor just kept moving. This had the effect of trapping all the people behind me. It all happened so fast. Within ten seconds, at least eight people had piled on top of me, and on each other as well. It soon became a crush as heads, arms and handbags draped all over me and the wheelchair, and over the sides of the escalator.

I looked up and saw everyone at the café staring, open-mouthed as the scene unfolded before them. A woman to my right, who was standing next to the large pillar, had wrapped her arms around it and was sinking to her knees in uproarious laughter.

My aunt, who was what you might call elderly, suddenly appeared to have the strength of ten men. She turned towards me, grabbed my wheelchair by the arms and somehow lifted me and the chair up, then set me down next to the escalator.

At this point everyone who had been trapped behind me fell to the ground in a heap of writhing bodies, with all of them trying to get up at the same time. It was bedlam. Thankfully, nobody was injured. Those who saw the funny side of the whole event were struggling to get up because they were laughing so hard.

In a matter of two minutes peace was restored again and everyone involved dispersed and went on their way. At that point, the people at the café started clapping. The woman hanging off the column called out to us that it was the funniest thing she had ever seen, yet she apologised at the same time for laughing at my predicament! My aunt and I decided that we would take the lift from now on and leave the escalators to more able-bodied individuals.

If I am ever in need of a pick-me-up, I remember that day, and the memory never fails to distract me from the situation at hand. Somehow, through this period of incapacity I enjoyed the funniest of moments, incidents I still remember to this day.

Soon I was mobile again, and the pain in my foot had gone. All that was left was a lovely long scar down the inside of my right foot which, to my surprise, has almost disappeared in the ensuing years.

When it was time to say goodbye to my wheelchair and return it to the Accident Compensation Corporation, our family decided to have a small party. I recall we were having a great time until the expected courier arrived to pick up the wheelchair and drive it to the depot which was at least two hours away in another city. As we stood in our doorway we cheered and clapped while the chair was loaded onto the truck. The courier clearly thought he had just visited the house of kooks as we waved and cheered at the departing van.

It was three days later when I heard a knock at the front door. We must have all heard it at the same time because our entire family went to open the door. There, at the door, stood a courier holding a large box. In it was my wheelchair! Somehow someone at the depot had seen our address on the box and didn't realise it was being returned, so they parcelled it up properly and sent it right back to us again!

As the courier stood there, one of our family pointed at the box and blurted out, "It's the wheelchair, it's come back again!"

At that, we all fell about laughing. It was so ridiculous. We had even had a party to say goodbye to the thing, and now it was back! It was like a boomerang. The courier clearly didn't know what to make of our reaction. All he saw was our family in fits of laughter. He had no idea of all we had been through leading up to that moment.

But it was over, it truly was over. We sent the wheelchair off again with the courier, and I continued with my day, walking once again without pain.

In life we can overcome some big obstacles and then, just like that wheelchair, the problem appears to return, a bit like a boomerang. We often have to fight for our miracles and breakthroughs. Sometimes we need to fight and fight and fight once more. But one thing we must never do, is give up. *Never give up.* You may not see it, but you are taking ground all the time, and eventually you will overcome in your situation until one day it has become but a dim memory. So, keep moving! Never give up hope, because one day you will have the victory.

- 20 -

Things are Going to Change

It was one of those summers that memories are made of—endless days filled with barbecues and swimming, followed by warm, balmy nights. It was January, and I was staying with Cameron and Kimberley, who were by now in their teens, at a large holiday park called *El Rancho* about an hour from our home. It was an annual pilgrimage for most of our family, as my sister Anne would stay with her family in a tent, my parents would be in their caravan, and our family would rent a unit in the lodge. Sometimes my other sister came with her family as well. There was a swimming pool, horses, a flying fox, canoes, and so much more. Our unit would generally be filled to overflowing with Cameron's friends who would bring their sleeping bags and stay with us as well. It was a wonderland of childhood memories and sunshine.

Geoff often stayed home to catch up with jobs around the house. Then he would drive up at the end of the week and relax with us. It was a summer to remember.

Little did I know that the bliss would soon come to an end and that we were about to enter a trial that would stretch us to our limits. I recall that last week at the holiday park because I had a sense God was trying to tell me something—about what, I didn't know, but I sensed it was some sort of warning. I would keep hearing something akin to a whisper being spoken to my heart, and it was always the same phrase, "Things are going to change; things are going to happen."

After hearing this several times over a period of a few days, I decided to share what I was hearing with Anne. I walked down the grassy path to her family's tent and stood with her in front of her picnic table and chairs. I told her that I kept hearing the words, "Things are going to change, things are going to happen," and I asked her what she thought they meant. Of course, she had no idea, but it felt good to share it with someone. We mulled it over for a while but came up with no answers and continued with our day.

The holiday was over all too soon, and we returned to our homes. The following Saturday I didn't feel well. I told Geoff that I was going to have a lie-down on the bed. To my surprise, about ten minutes later Geoff walked in and lay down on the bed beside me. He said he didn't feel well either. I am embarrassed to say I was secretly a little pleased about this, because Geoff seemed to have superhuman resistance to bugs. I thought how great it was that for once he had caught the same thing as me. I recall asking him what he was feeling, and I remember his reply being a little odd.

"I just feel strange," he said.

Well, that was very different to me. I felt like I had a weak virus, but I certainly didn't feel 'strange'. *Never mind*, I thought, *his description is just a bit lacking. He must mean he feels like he has a virus.*

The following day I woke at 7a.m. to the most blood-curdling sound. I remember opening my eyes and asking myself what on earth that sound could be. I turned to look at Geoff and realised it was coming from him! His eyes were closed, and he was making a peculiar-sounding, high-pitched noise, almost like a scream. I jumped onto my knees and shook him, but he didn't wake up. The screaming was shrill and terrifying.

I grabbed the phone and dialled 111. I tried to tell the lady at the other end of the phone what was happening, but I was finding it difficult to get my words out. Thankfully, she didn't need convincing—she could hear Geoff loud and clear through the phone. She told me not to hang up, but I said I wanted to throw some trackpants and a sweatshirt on, and I wanted to ring my sister who lived nearby. The lady then told me an ambulance was on its way and she would call me back within two minutes. During that time, I threw on some clothes and rang my sister Anne, asking her to come and help.

By this time, Geoff had opened his eyes. His pupils were huge and staring at nothing. He started to thrash so much that I couldn't get near him. Kimberley had got up and was waiting for the ambulance at the front door. Cameron was staying with a friend so wasn't at home that night.

In no time at all the first of three ambulances arrived. We lived in a small cul-de-sac, and it was soon lined with ambulances. Then my sister and her husband, Graeme, arrived. It's funny how obscure things can stay in your mind, things that bear no relevance to the situation at hand. I remember Anne had a coat on, and I could see her nightgown hanging down well below the hemline of the coat.

The bedroom was now filled with paramedics. I stood at the end of the bed feeling somewhat disconnected from what was going on. Geoff was still unconscious, and convulsing so violently that the paramedics were all trying to help each other hold him down.

Then another paramedic arrived in the bedroom holding what looked to me like an enormous syringe. Turning to me, he said, "If he doesn't calm down, I am going to give him the elephant dose!"

Whether he gave it to him or not I can't recall, but I can still see my brother-in-law sitting on the bed trying to hold Geoff down. I was useless and just stood there. At that moment I heard the Holy Spirit speak to me above all the noise, "The thing that was going to happen has happened, and now things are going to change."

I was petrified. *What was wrong with Geoff? Was he going to die? Was he going to be an invalid?* I didn't know.

Finally, after what seemed like forever, they managed to get Geoff strapped onto a stretcher and carried to the ambulance. I asked Graeme to come in the back of the ambulance with me as I felt dazed and unable to think straight.

At this point the wild thrashing behaviour had ceased but Geoff still wasn't conscious. We departed for Wellington Hospital.

I remember looking out of the ambulance window as we drove along beside the sea which was next to the highway. It wasn't my first time in the back of an ambulance. I had been a passenger myself several times, as had my parents and my mother-in-law. So it wasn't a new experience for me, yet it was still all rather surreal.

It was strange to see cars on the road, and people going about their business. Some were no doubt looking forward to some retail therapy, while others would have been heading to church. For them it was just another Sunday, while for me, my world had just turned upside down.

As the ambulance approached the emergency department, Geoff started to regain consciousness. No one knew what to say, and I remember Graeme joking with Geoff, although Geoff didn't say much back. It's funny how, when something traumatic happens, we as humans just make jokes with one another. It's like we need to let off steam to lighten the moment. It was good because I didn't know what to say.

Soon Geoff was parked on a bed in the accident and emergency department. I had worked in accident and emergency as a nurse, but when it's your own family member who is a patient it's very different, very different indeed. The doctor came and asked Geoff some questions: *What year is it? What day is it? Who is the prime minister?* I can no longer remember Geoff's answers, but I remember looking at his face and thinking he didn't look well at all.

Geoff was admitted to a ward for further investigations, and I went home to shower and see Kimberley. By the time I got home, word had spread that something had happened to Geoff, and the phone was ringing off the hook. We were told that friends from across different churches were praying—Catholics, Salvationists, Baptists, Pentecostals, the lot.

Geoff had scans and blood tests but was sent home later that week because he insisted he could travel into hospital for further tests if need be. Those days were tough because Geoff didn't know what we had seen and gone through, and he tried to minimise the whole event. It soon became evident that Geoff wasn't the same. For a start, his skin had a grey pallor, his eyes were vague, and he was very tired.

But that was only the beginning. I immediately noticed that he was repeating sentences and then forgetting he ever said them. Geoff had always had a brilliant mind and a photographic memory, and to be honest, I was scared. I hoped it would pass quickly, and it did improve but it didn't go away.

Because Geoff wasn't allowed to drive until a diagnosis had been made, I had to drive him everywhere. If you want to find an almost sure recipe for divorce, get your husband's licence taken away and become the sole driver. It appeared that Geoff had forgotten that I had been driving for many years and decided I now required hand signals at every corner and intersection. His frustration was evident as was mine, and at times I thought I might throttle him.

Soon Geoff returned to his work as the deputy principal of a large secondary school. To me he clearly wasn't ready, but it's hard to convince someone who has no real grasp on how unwell they were because they were unconscious at the time. Because Geoff had no memory of the event, he insisted on going to work rather than taking sick leave while he underwent further investigations.

I drove Geoff to his tests and waited around, hoping for an answer. After an electroencephalogram (otherwise known as an EEG), we were told Geoff wasn't an epileptic. His other tests all came back negative as well. We were told that it could have been a blood clot in the brain, but no one was sure. There were many possibilities but no exact diagnosis.

Still, I was living with someone who now forgot a lot of what I said and repeated his sentences. Soon I began receiving messages from Geoff's work colleagues who reported the same things to me, saying he wasn't working to full capacity, that he was repetitive and forgetting things. I was getting really concerned. *What if Geoff had to leave his job?* I was imagining all sorts of horrific outcomes.

It all came to a head one Wednesday around three months after the incident. I was so exhausted I could barely function. I was trying to stay positive despite my own health issues, but now with Geoff as well, it was a lot to carry.

We had met with a neurologist who told us that at the end of the day there might not be a definite diagnosis, and what happened to Geoff might just be an unexplainable event. He also told us that a scan had revealed what appeared to be a lesion on his brain and that it might have been there his entire life, or it could be connected to the incident. The plan was that we would continue with regular appointments to monitor the situation.

We drove away from the hospital perplexed. In some ways the results were good but in another way, it left us hanging in the air. *Was it going to happen again? Would Geoff just get better?* After dealing with the situation for what now felt like forever, I just wanted to go home and sleep for a week.

I remember it was a lovely autumn day and once more Geoff had insisted on going to work after a specialist appointment. He was attending a conference in a nearby town, so I dropped him off there. I recall feeling empty inside, tired and alone.

I needed to do some banking, so I called in at the local bank. Standing in the queue, I turned to see someone I knew from church. I'm sure I tried to hide—I felt too weary to talk and just wanted to go home. But she had seen me first and was waiting for me after I finished my banking.

Tracey Marshall is one of those people that you notice. Her hair was a little like a lion's mane in colour and was just as magnificent. She was petite and pretty with an endearing smile. She was also honest and not afraid to give you the hard word if that is what you needed to hear. I had worked with her sister, Sandra, at the Open Home Foundation. In appearance, Tracey couldn't have been more different to Sandra, although they were both very attractive women, and they both had the same passion for God.

So there was Tracey, in the bank, waiting to have a chat with me. When I got close to her, she immediately asked if I was doing okay. I must have looked terrible for her to say that. I guess my face said it all, and she asked me to walk with her. I was so touched by her kindness that I decided walking with her was better than going home and feeling sorry for myself.

We walked past shops and cafés and various other places until we came to an outdoor area. I noticed a metallic sign had been placed on the concrete. It read: Women's Aglow Upstairs. *Oh*, I thought, *they must have left their sign out and gone home.* It was now after 12.30 p.m. and I knew that this group met in the mornings and would have finished by now. I remembered Women's Aglow fondly from the time they had prayed with me. This was clearly a branch of the same group.

I was about to keep walking, but Tracey said she thought we should go upstairs to where the sign pointed. I told her I was sure they had already finished and left the sign out by mistake, but Tracey was determined and started to climb the narrow stairs to the first floor. Having no expectation of anything, I decided to follow her if only to see whether someone was still upstairs so we could notify them they had forgotten their sign.

At the top of the stairs we were met by a short, narrow hallway lined with closed doors. Tracey knocked on the first door on the right. I was standing behind her feeling slightly foolish and wondering how my quick trip to the bank had turned into this.

At that moment, a lady opened the door. Quite matter-of-factly, she welcomed us into a room where eight to ten ladies, mostly Pacific Island and Māori, but a few Pakeha (the name given to white inhabitants of New Zealand) as well, sat on chairs in a circle. This kind lady proceeded to inform us they had been waiting for us.

They had been waiting for us? Who were these people? I had never seen any of them before in my life, and they were waiting for me? One lady, who clearly was the leader, proceeded to tell us that God had spoken to them about a woman with a great need, and that they were to wait and pray until she came.

I was dumbfounded. God had done this for me? I'd felt invisible, broken and alone, and now this lady was telling me they were waiting for me? It was the most wonderful moment. I was still weary and burdened with what I had been dealing with for the past few months, but now I had hope.

The ladies gathered around me. I briefly told them about my situation but they didn't seem hung up on any details; they knew God had it all in hand. They then started to pray. Together they prayed, all these ladies from different races lifting Geoff up to God in unison.

I was so tired I just stood there and did nothing. I was just glad for them to pray.

They continued to pray for about twenty minutes, and then it was over. Lifting my head, I opened my eyes and saw them putting their coats on and getting their handbags. They were going to have lunch in the nearby mall and asked if we would like to join them, so we did. As we sat with our new friends and shared a light meal, I felt as if I had known these ladies for half my life. They were so welcoming and kind, and I really enjoyed their company.

When it was time to go our separate ways, I looked at Tracey. She had let God use her, and as a result, something wonderful happened that I remember to this day.

When I got home the tiredness felt the same, but I had enough strength to ring some friends and Geoff to tell them about this amazing encounter. That evening when I drove to pick up Geoff, I was looking forward to seeing if there had been any change. There was! It wasn't radical, but I could see a light in his eyes that hadn't been there before. The next day there was substantial improvement.

By Friday I had my husband back. He was once again the sharp-minded person he had always been. The forgetfulness was gone, and he was the old Geoff again. It was wonderful. To me it was a miracle. Only those who were living with him could see the fullness of what God had done in Geoff, but he was healed!

That same Friday afternoon I received a phone call from the radiologist. He proceeded to inform me that a specialist from Australia had just reviewed Geoff's brain scan. He could find no evidence of a brain lesion, and the scan appeared normal.

I hung up the phone stunned. *How could this be? Was it read incorrectly in the first place? Had there been a mistake?* I didn't care. There was no lesion. This was wonderful news.

Standing in my dining room looking across at the bush which covered the nearby hill, I tried to process all that had happened in the last three days. I had gone from despair to great joy. I couldn't explain it all, but I didn't care. Geoff was well again.

A couple of months later, Geoff's improvement was so remarkable that the doctor relented, at Geoff's persistence, and gave him permission to drive once more. My joy knew no bounds. My plans to throttle him were put on hold. It was now July, and he was permitted to drive to work again.

I wrote a letter to the women at the Aglow group to thank them for praying for our family and tell them of Geoff's remarkable recovery. They gave me their prayers, their time, their love and kindness, and expected nothing in return.

I don't know if they still meet, and I wouldn't recognise them after that fleeting encounter, but I salute them and Tracey for being there for me that day. I hope that if you ever need prayer, others will be there to lift you up as well. Or in turn you could be the one to lift others up in their time of need.

- 21 -

A Blessing

I was in the middle of doing housework one day when I felt a prompting from God. It came from nowhere and it wasn't related to anything I was thinking or doing. Without explanation or apparent reason, I heard the words, "I am going to give you a house."

I stopped what I was doing. I remember I was holding a toilet brush in my hand, as I was cleaning the bathroom at the time. I've long learned that God is less hung up on formality and ceremony than we are, and He will speak to us anywhere and at any time and in any way He chooses.

I stood there half doubting that I had actually heard anything. Maybe I had made it up, or maybe it was my overactive imagination. It made no sense. We had a house. I liked it. It was a very nice house in a lovely street. We had a mortgage, but I never gave that a second thought because that was normal for most families.

I decided to chalk up the experience to my imagination. But just in case it wasn't, I told two trusted friends. That way, if it ever came to anything, they could confirm that I had said God had spoken to me. I also gave them permission to have a laugh at my expense if it all came to nothing.

About six weeks passed. The memory of the "I am going to give you a house" incident was starting to fade. And then, I started to have a niggling thought. It was rather a bizarre thought and didn't make a lot of sense, but it kept getting louder in my mind—the following Sunday, our church was collecting a special offering for overseas missionaries, and, much like I felt when I knew I was to give the money for my birthday ring to Te Mona, I kept having a strong feeling that we were to empty our bank account of all our savings and give the lot to the special missionary collection at church.

Now at the time, we were struggling financially. We always had enough, but in truth, we were just scraping by. I never felt hard done by, as again and again I saw quite miraculous provision in our lives, but to clear out our bank account was a whole other thing.

If someone ever shared with me that they had the same notion, I would caution them to think carefully. Sometimes God gives people what is called a *'rhema'* word. This is a specific instruction just for you. It's not for anyone else—just you. It doesn't mean that everyone should act on the same instruction. The word should also line up with the Bible, otherwise it is not from God. For instance, if someone told me God was encouraging them to steal some equipment from their employer, or abuse someone online who was annoying them, I would confidently remind them that this is not how God works. In other words, be sure you know that what you are hearing or feeling is correct, or you could land yourself in hot water.

In this case, I knew my 'niggling feeling' was more than just that—it was a *rhema* word. And so, on Thursday that week, I shared with Geoff what I was feeling we should do with our savings. Now in reality it wasn't a lot of money, but when you don't have a lot, every dollar counts. To my surprise, Geoff didn't look at me as if I had lost my mind and agreed to go with what I was feeling.

Over the next few days, the urge to keep the money was strong, but we didn't. When Sunday came around, I told the family I wanted to meet in the lounge before church. I had our savings in cash in an envelope. We stood in a little huddle and prayed a simple prayer. I remember asking God to take care of our finances and help us make ends meet. I prayed an honest prayer from the heart, and then it was over. That morning, we put that envelope in the missionary collection, and after church we went back home.

A BLESSING

The following day at 9 a.m., just twenty-four hours after we had prayed with the family over the money in the envelope, I was doing housework once again when I heard the phone ringing. On the other end of the phone, a man introduced himself as an employee of the Accident Compensation Corporation. He explained that my doctor had, unbeknown to me, applied for a compensation payment related to my foot injury and the effects it had had on my life and my job. He was calling to ask for a bank account number into which he could deposit the money. The amount was in the thousands.

I hung up the phone completely stunned. Then it hit me. I had never had so much money in my life! I literally fell on my knees. *Was this really happening?* I thought God might assist us make ends meet, but I never expected this!

That night I told our children and Geoff what had happened, and we thanked God for His amazing provision. Little did I know it was only the beginning.

I was blessed with a lovely mother-in-law. As time passed, she started to have some health issues, so the family helped relocate her to a retirement village not far from our home. She was free to come and go, but had her needs met and meals provided. It worked out very well for her. I soon developed a habit of picking her up every time I went out, and she would be with me for the day, then I would drop her off sometime in the afternoon. She was a delight to have around and good company. Over the years, we enjoyed sharing morning teas together at just about every café in or near our town.

The day after receiving word of the compensation payment for my foot, I went out early and as usual, picked up Grandma (as we called her) on my way. We were sitting in a café later that morning when she started talking to me about Geoff's aunt who had remained single all her life and lived in England. Geoff's father had always been very good to her and sent her regular payments throughout her adult life.

Grandma proceeded to tell me there was a large set of silver cutlery that had the family initials engraved on every piece and was currently with the aunt in England. Grandma told me that when this aunt passed away, she wanted Geoff to inherit this silverware. It was an interesting conversation and I told Grandma I would mention it to Geoff when he came home from work that night. Thinking nothing more about it, we continued with our day.

Geoff arrived home from work earlier than usual that afternoon. We were all still riding high on the excitement of the compensation, and there was an air of happiness in the house. As we sat in the lounge, I asked Geoff if he knew anything about the silverware that Grandma had told me about that morning. He could not recall ever hearing about it before, so that was about the extent of our conversation.

That afternoon at four o'clock, the phone rang. It was the lady who had purchased Grandma's house when Grandma moved into the retirement village. She had received a large envelope in the mail from England and asked if we could please pick it up. Ten minutes later we were driving down the highway to collect the envelope.

Arriving home a short time later, we saw that the envelope appeared to contain legal documents so we rang Grandma and asked her what she wanted us to do with it. She wanted us to open it.

Inside the envelope was a letter from a lawyer in England informing Grandma that her late husband's sister had passed away. Along with the letter was a copy of her will. Sure enough, a set of silver cutlery with the family initials on each piece had been bequeathed to Geoff—the very set Grandma had told me about that morning. I had shared that information with Geoff, and only an hour later, we received this news! Was this another God-incident?! It certainly was! But that wasn't all. On reading further, it became apparent that Geoff's aunt had owned her own home in England, and on her death she wanted it sold and the money divided between Geoff, his brother, and his mother. We sat on the couch and just stared at the document before us.

Were we part of a movie? This felt like the sort of thing you hear about but it doesn't happen to you. And yet . . . now it was! Geoff had a sad look on his face and I knew I should feel a bit sorrowful too, even though his aunt had lived a long and happy life. I did in a way, but there was no denying that this was going to change our lives. Neither of us really knew how to behave at first, but when reality hit, we let ourselves enjoy the moment. We had gone from having no savings at all to receiving a compensation pay-out of thousands, and then within another twenty-four hours we had inherited an estate of many thousands! We agreed to use the money to purchase a new home.

It may sound a little presumptuous, but we went out with a real estate agent to look at some houses that same week. The first house we saw was very grand and not something I ever imagined owning. It was only a year old and sat at the top of a hill in a fairly new subdivision with lovely views of the surrounding district and hills in the distance. The owners were looking for a lifestyle change and had purchased a motel, which involved leaving the district.

After viewing this house, I sat in the car, staring up and admiring it. It was truly beautiful. Our daughter then commented matter-of-factly, "I know this house, and I love it! When I am on the bus travelling to college, we go down this street. As we drive past I've been asking God if we could live in it one day."

I turned in the car and looked at her. *Was she joking?* But she wasn't.

It was almost too much to take in. Within a few days of receiving the news of the inheritance, we had our eye on a new home and a new car and were looking forward to fulfilling Geoff's lifetime dream of owning a boat. We also discussed giving money away to various charities and causes we wanted to support.

It all seems so far-fetched now, but that is how it happened. We worked out how much money we would be likely to receive, and we had based our search for a house on that. We decided to borrow from the bank to cover the mortgage until the inheritance arrived—rather like bridging finance. I asked God to confirm that this was what He wanted us to do with the inheritance money by allowing our current house to sell quickly, and for cash. Sure enough, we put it on the market, and it sold for cash in two days, which was unheard of at that time.

The following week, however, we started having second thoughts. Was it really the right thing to do, to buy a house before the inheritance arrived? Our minds started swirling. There was almost an expectation of everything coming crashing down around us. The week before I had known so clearly that we were meant to buy a house. Now I started overthinking everything. But we kept moving forward and sure enough, our offer on the house on top of the hill was accepted.

I have been through many hardships in my life, mostly relating to my health and Geoff's, but there have been other things as well. There is a Bible verse that says God "restores the years the locusts have eaten." It's true, and it happened to us. My problems didn't disappear overnight, and I wasn't instantaneously healed—I still had a few surgeries ahead—but God lifted our financial burden for that season, and that meant a lot.

I remember the day our family walked into that house knowing it was ours! On the first floor was a large lounge and dining room, open plan kitchen, and family room. There was also a sort of 'hangout area', a bathroom and toilet, and three bedrooms, one of which was huge and had its own ensuite. In a separate wing of the house was the master bedroom, also with an ensuite and walk-in wardrobe, along with a study and a laundry.

I can still see Cameron and Kimberley running as fast as they could to the large bedroom upstairs. I bounded up the stairs behind them to see what they were up to.

Cameron beat Kimberley by a couple of seconds, and as he entered the big bedroom he yelled, "Shotgun!" I soon learned this meant, 'Got here first, so it's mine!' And it was. From the day we moved in, Cameron would often be entertaining a crowd in that room. Kimberley was good humoured about it all and took residence in a smaller bedroom.

A BLESSING

We were enjoying our new home, but six months after moving in, the money we had borrowed for the mortgage payments ran out and the inheritance had still not arrived. We were stuck. I remember standing in Cameron's bedroom with him and Kimberley. They were teenagers, so I figured they could handle it when I told them we had no money left.

Once again, I found myself doubting our decision to buy this house. I imagined us slinking off as a family as the mockers pelted us with phrases such as, "You idiots! Some God you believe in!", or "Serves you right, you fools."

The only thing we had, was prayer. So that day, the three of us prayed. I guess I sounded rather desperate. I reminded God that we had taken this step out of what we considered obedience, and that it was not right for Him to lead us to buy the house only to have to sell it again after six months. I asked Him to make a way. Then our prayer-time was over.

The three of us headed out to the car. We were about to do the grocery shopping with the little money we had left, and I was feeling rather despondent. It seemed there was no quick way out of our financial situation. I backed the car out of the garage, then stopped to check the letterbox before we headed on our way. Inside was an envelope, and since there was nothing to indicate who it was from, I opened it right there and then.

Inside was a letter with another piece of paper attached. I took a quick look and saw it was a cheque for $66,000! I literally started shaking. Even now it is a large sum of money, but at that time, to us, it was huge. I could hardly read the attached letter. It was an inheritance from another estate within our family! There had been no indication that this money was coming, and I could hardly believe my eyes. We all started screaming with joy and jubilation! Anyone passing by would have thought we were drunk, we were so loud. Less than five minutes beforehand we had prayed for God to rescue us, and now we had received way more than we needed to tide us over until the money arrived to pay the mortgage off. It was the biggest cheque I had seen in my life!

Eventually we calmed down and I realised we needed to get to the bank to deposit the cheque before the bank closed. I remember driving along the road waving the cheque in the air and yelling out to Cameron and Kimberley, "This is not normal. Don't think that God is a money tree—this is not normal." I didn't want my children to go through life thinking God was some sort of slot machine. I wanted them to understand that God was our provider but that He also expects us to work and earn and save our money, and not just expect Him to give us loot when we wanted it. Still, it truly was an incredible moment, and I will always be thankful for that season of provision in our lives.

I remember the day the inheritance finally arrived along with a shipping container with various pieces of furniture from England. Our hearts were full of thankfulness and joy. It was now a year since we had given all our money to the missionary fund. Now here we were in this beautiful home with the mortgage paid off, and I had my car, and Geoff, his boat. I truly believe that God not only grieves with us when we grieve, but He enjoys our happiness too. He experiences the emotional ups and downs of life with us.

It was the most wonderful feeling to donate thousands to various causes as we had planned, including funding wells in Africa. By the time it was over we didn't have a bulging bank account, but we didn't have debts either and we had a nice lifestyle.

Months after we had finally settled into our new surroundings, I was walking up the hill towards our new home. I was on the other side of the street from our house. Two men who lived on the same street with their families were chatting and looking over towards our house.

I stopped to say a friendly hello, and they told me they had just been discussing our family. One of the men then asked me (with a reasonably serious expression on his face) if we were drug dealers! Taken aback, I asked what made him say that. He replied that they couldn't understand how we could afford a house like ours when

I didn't work (of course, he didn't know anything about my health or life), Geoff was a teacher, and we were still reasonably young. I was amazed that this had even entered their heads, let alone their conversation.

The men went on to say they had seen a man pull up at our house in a van a couple of times each week and leave a large sack hidden on our deck. I burst out laughing. Because our house was at the top of a hill, the manager of the local post office had asked if a bag of mail could be left at our property every few days so the mailman wouldn't have to carry it all the way up the hill. When he got to our house, he could simply pick up the bag and continue his mail round. Drug dealers indeed!

This experience, although funny, taught me that I had to be careful how I shared about the events of the past year and a half. At first, I would just blurt out that God had given us this house. But my explanation was often met with laughter, or a look that said, 'weirdo', or disbelief. It wasn't coming across as the great testimony of God's goodness I thought it would be. I realised I had to be careful what I said, how I said it, and who I said it to.

God carries us through the dark times and is with us in the good times. He is a faithful provider. But not everybody's journey is the same. All of us are believing God for different things. The years have passed, and since then we have moved to different parts of New Zealand. Our current house is not as grand, but it's cosy and it is home. I often look back at this time in our lives and am reminded of God's goodness and provision throughout every season of our lives.

- 22 -

Lifting my Burden

One day, I was pushing my mother in a wheelchair when I felt an awful pain in my upper back. It was as if I was being ripped apart. I was in agony. In time, normality returned—except for one thing. If I ever tried to lift a heavy box or a weighty bag of groceries, I would get a pounding headache. This would last for a few days and then settle down again. The resulting injury caused me to leave my job, and for months all I could do for much of the day was rest on my bed.

I soon learned to live this way and it became my new normal. It's funny how, if a situation comes upon you slowly, you are more likely to accept it because in its sneakiness you never realise it's getting worse until it ensnares you.

The years passed, and I avoided lifting anything heavy. If I ever forgot, I would soon be back in bed nursing another headache. I'd had physiotherapy and tried other treatments, but in the end, accepted that this was how life was going to be from now on. Although I had put up with the pain for years, I got to the point where I didn't have the mental ability to deal with it anymore.

One day, I was ruminating about the pain in my back. I was over it. We were meant to be moving house the next day, but I knew that if I lifted one thing that was too heavy for me, the unpacking would be ruined by a pounding headache. I had grouched my way around the house all morning, and it was a blessing no one else was home as

I don't think I was great company.

Sitting on the couch that afternoon, I started talking with God. I talked to Him about my back, and how I didn't think I could cope with this for the rest of my life. I talked about the following day and how I was expected to unpack boxes and how difficult it was going to be. Then I turned the television on.

Have you ever watched Christian television? It can be a mixed bag, ranging from beautiful music to painful screeching depending on your taste and the channel you are watching at the time. I've listened to some diabolical speakers, and to the most impactful and powerful preachers who know God in a deep way. It's a 'pick and choose' of all things Christian.

On this particular afternoon, there was a show on television called *The 700 Club*. There was a small segment of the programme that consisted of a man and a woman praying for viewers.

Now I have no doubt that the prayers being prayed that day were for many people. After all, so many suffer ailments that are common to all mankind. I switched on the television to hear the following words, "There is a woman watching this show today and she has a back injury that she has been praying about. God is healing her right now. Just receive His healing touch."

Suddenly I sat to attention. *Could this be me?* Not knowing what I should do, I think I may have said something like, "I receive my healing," but in truth I can't remember. What I do clearly remember, is that as soon as they prayed, I felt something.

In the middle of my spine, halfway up my back, I began to feel heat. It was as if a small fire had been lit inside my spine. Then slowly this sensation of heat began to grow. It started to move downward to the bottom of my spine and upward to the top of my neck. As it moved, it got hotter until I felt as if my spine was on fire! It wasn't painful, but it was intense. It didn't take me long to realise my back was being healed!

Not sure what I should be doing, I just sat on the couch for a while. My eyes filled with tears as all the emotions attached to the years of pain started to be released. I expected that at any moment the heat would disappear, but it didn't. It remained for an hour and a half. I walked through the house, amazed at the timing. A sense of happiness filled me as I realised, I was going to be able to unpack my belongings the next day without the fear of a headache!

I soon told my family and close friends what had happened, and they all shared in my joy. The next day my back felt different—the pain and tension were completely gone.

From that day on the headaches that came from the back injury ceased. I could carry boxes and do normal things once again. It has now been a number of years since this healing, and I have had occasional discomfort in my back when I overdo things. But the pain related to the years of heavy lifting and the resulting headaches have never come back.

I have watched those same people on *The 700 Club* pray for other conditions over the years since that healing. I have stretched out my hands towards them when they have prayed for sinus conditions and other ailments, and nothing has happened for me at the time. Again and again I have had to accept that God is not a 'one size fits all' healer. We cannot box Him into our narrow field of vision. My sinuses are now healed, but it was through surgery.

God will do what is right for you. Some are never healed, and I don't have the answers. But once again, I encourage you: never give up; never, never give up, because you never know what is waiting for you just around the corner.

- 23 -

Heartbeat

After the birth of my children, I developed a condition which led to my blood pressure being very high. This produced all sorts of effects—my heart often pounded loudly as it struggled to cope, and I began getting headaches so intense that I could not always drive safely or reliably. I always believed that in time healing would come. In the meantime, however, my job required driving to various clients, so I made the decision to step down and focus on my health.

By now I had spent so many hours in hypertension clinics and the cardiology outpatient department that I was easily recognised by various members of staff. I knew pharmacists like they were old friends. But the medications prescribed to control my blood pressure only had minimal effect.

My father experienced similar difficulty controlling his blood pressure and had surgery on his heart, but apart from that instance in our family history, there seemed to be no obvious cause for this problem. I was careful with my diet, not overweight, reasonably fit, and not unduly stressed. And yet routine ECG's showed considerable thickening of the walls of my heart, and at times my blood pressure would rise to 210/110, which was concerning to my cardiologist.

Having lived with this condition for years, I had somewhat given up hope of a resolution. Still, I finally accepted that grumbling my way through life with a chip on my shoulder because of my health wasn't a great advertisement for the Christian life.

My children had dealt with my blood pressure and its drama all their lives. Now they had grown up and were independent. Cameron had relocated to Wellington to study at university after my parents' once beloved home was sold. He was now working in information technology.

Kimberley was now married to the most wonderful man, and we were so pleased to welcome him into our lives. Aaron Te Whaiti soon became part of our family. He accepted that with our family came sudden outbursts of prayer, and that we talked about God as if He were sitting in the room with us. It takes a special person to accept us on that level. Aaron is that person.

Geoff and I had moved into our third house since the original blessing of the house on the hill. I was sad that Opa and Oma never got to see our new house as I'm sure they would have loved it. This house had expansive sea views and was surrounded in decking, with a large brick barbeque in the middle of the deck.

Over the years my blood pressure had continued to deteriorate, and I was getting concerned that if it didn't come under control, I might have a stroke. A number of years earlier, after a lengthy session of headaches and vomiting, I'd appeared to have had some kind of self-resolving (thankfully) mini stroke while shopping with my sister Anne at a local mall. On that occasion I felt the sensation on one side of my body leaving me. I was already in a wheelchair because I was still weak from being sick, which turned out to be a good thing. Anne drove me to the medical centre, but by then I had lost all feeling down one side of my body and was unable to move it. The doctor called for an ambulance, and I went back into hospital.

My children and my nieces and nephews were so immune to seeing me being taken to hospital that they approached the whole situation with great hilarity. I can still see Anne following the ambulance with all the children crammed into the car. At one point they overtook the ambulance, and I could see them through the window while I lay on the stretcher. The windows of Anne's car were wound down, and my children along with their cousins were hanging out of the car windows waving their arms wildly and screaming my name and rollicking with laughter.

Even then I could see the funny side of the situation, and I believe God guarded their hearts. Somehow they knew it would always work out okay, and it did. Thankfully, my feeling quickly returned, and within twenty-four hours I was back home. I still remembered that experience, however, and never wanted it to recur, especially not as a full-blown stroke.

One Sunday, not too long after we had moved into our new home, for no apparent reason I felt strongly we should watch the regular Sunday night documentary programme on television. So, we switched it on.

That night, the documentary was about a relatively new procedure called renal denervation. It was being trialled on people who were resistant to antihypertensive medication, and so far, the results were promising. The procedure targeted the renal nerves, which in turn affect blood pressure.

I remember Geoff and I just staring at each other. *Was this my lifeline? Could this be for me?* I realised that I was getting older and that my body couldn't sustain such extreme hypertension for much longer. We agreed that I would see my local doctor as soon as possible and ask him to find out more.

The next day I sat in my doctor's office excitedly talking about the documentary and what I had seen. The doctor hadn't seen it but said he would make enquiries. This turned into quite a mission. Renal denervation was still a relatively new procedure in New Zealand at the time and was only being carried out at Mercy Hospital in Auckland, eight hours drive from Wellington, where we lived. My doctor held discussions with the specialist in Auckland, and soon I was accepted as a potential candidate for the procedure.

A short time later, Geoff and I would fly to Auckland for further testing before it would be decided if I was a suitable candidate. Unbeknown to me, I was about to go on a journey that would involve a lot more than a renal denervation.

I was rather excited in the weeks following my visit to my doctor. Hope accounts for a lot, and I now had plenty of it. On the week I was due to fly to Auckland, my good friends Viv and Mel came to my house to pray for me before I left.

I was preparing the morning tea before their arrival when a loud banging came from somewhere in the house. I followed the sound down my hallway and discovered it was coming from my laundry. I figured the load of washing I had placed in the machine had become unbalanced and was causing my machine to make the banging noise.

I opened the bifold doors to the small room that housed my washing machine, tub, and dryer. To my surprise, not only was my washing machine banging wildly around, but a plug had fallen into the adjacent tub, blocking the drainage hole.

I turned off the washing machine and quickly pulled out the plug which was keeping the water from draining, just in time to prevent a flood in my laundry. At that moment I felt God say to me: "The unbalanced washing machine and the blockage in the tub stopping the water draining are a depiction of what is happening to you and your heart."

I stepped back. *What on earth did that mean?* I decided to ask Viv and Mel, hoping they might shed some light on how the blocked tub and out-of-kilter washing machine related to my own health situation.

When Mel and Viv arrived we settled into our leather chairs as we always did, enjoying a drink and something to eat. The chairs faced the sea, and it was a lovely place to sit—a good place for rest and recuperation as I recovered from whatever lay ahead. That day, however, neither Mel nor Viv could think what the words I had heard might mean, so we agreed to take one step at a time and see if something unfolded that would help make sense of what God had spoken.

On the day we were to depart for Auckland the weather was bad, and it was touch and go whether we would be able to fly out at all. But in the end, we got away and made it to our destination.

Arriving in Auckland, we were met by a taxi and taken to a hotel that had been booked by hospital staff. That night we got little sleep as a gentleman in the room above us was on the phone all night, yelling in a foreign language. Every time we rang reception he quieted down for a while, and then he would be off yelling at the top of his voice once more.

Morning finally came. A taxi arrived, and we were driven to Mercy Hospital's angiography unit for a series of tests. The excitement combined with very little sleep was a great recipe for an abnormal blood pressure reading, even for those who never suffered from hypertension. Sure enough, my blood pressure, which was now off the charts, clearly indicated that something was amiss. I was then sent for a renal scan.

Once the initial tests were over, Geoff and I were ushered into a room with others who were there for the same reason as me. I didn't feel as if I was in a waiting room. It felt like a giant filing cabinet that had been hurriedly made into a waiting room. What appeared to be medical records were piled high on metal shelving almost up to the ceiling, and there was an assortment of chairs for people to sit on while they waited to meet with the specialist.

Looking around the room, I began to think I had been hoodwinked. It looked more like a waiting room to find out who had been accepted into a retirement village for the elderly. I was the youngest in that room by at least twenty years!

One by one people were being called into the specialist's office. Then it was my turn. Being so much younger and by all appearances somewhat fitter than the other candidates, I was fully expecting that I would be accepted immediately for the procedure.

We entered a somewhat darkened room with computer screens on desks. The specialist called us over and pointed at a screen showing a CT scan of someone's renal arteries and asked us what we saw.

In truth, I just saw a bunch of arteries, and it didn't make a lot of sense to me. He then explained what we were looking at. This was my CT scan, and it showed severe narrowing at the origin of the left renal artery, a condition known as renal stenosis. This artery carries oxygen-rich blood to the kidneys, which enables them to filter waste products and remove excess fluids. When the renal arteries are blocked, the outcome is fluid retention, shortness of breath, and possible kidney failure.

Geoff and I just stood staring at the screen. We were both so surprised. The stenosis was secondary to malignant hypertension! Then I came up with an idea. It seemed reasonable to me that the radiographer had mixed up my scan with one of the more elderly patients in the waiting room. Embarrassingly, I dared to step back and tell the specialist there was a mistake. There had been a mix up. This couldn't be me, it had to belong to one of the senior citizens in the waiting room. He took this with good humour. He told us he would personally walk to the other side of the hospital to check this out with the radiographer, and sure enough, off he went. Twenty minutes later, he was back. No, there had been no mistake—the CT scan was mine.

The timing of this scan was nothing short of a life-saver for me. The specialist told us that ordinarily the stenosis would make me unsuitable for a renal denervation. But this was a God-moment in the making. He went on to say that he had seen a case in Europe where a stenosis had been dilated with a balloon, allowing renal denervation to be carried out in that renal artery and a stent implanted. This approach was not standard practice, but he wanted to consider it for me because of the severity of my blood pressure problems.

First, however, I had to be examined by a renal physician back in Wellington. This physician would determine if I was a good candidate for this intervention. Feeling a little deflated but realising I really had no choice, we decided to move forward with this plan.

∼

I believe it was the following day when the situation with the washing machine and the blocked tub suddenly came back to me and I had my "you've got to be kidding" moment. My heart was the struggling and out-of-balance washing machine, the plug blocking the flow was the stenosis, and the flooding tub was my kidneys! I was amazed! Now it all made total sense. It was enough to encourage me as we took the next step.

Back in Wellington I saw the renal physician, who recommended an angioplasty and stenting of my left renal artery, followed by a bilateral renal denervation. It was all coming together, and once again I was feeling hopeful. In just a short time, Geoff and I would set off back to Auckland for the big event.

That's when things started to go a little awry. Geoff began seeing what appeared to be a shadow moving down over his right eye. He took himself off to the emergency doctor and was sent home with a diagnosis of possible eye infection and told to come back if it got worse. Over a period of a few days, the problem worsened. This time Geoff went to the emergency department of our local hospital, and within hours he was having surgery for a detached retina. Once more, it was a miracle of timing. His vision was saved, but now he was unable to fly to Auckland.

So it was that I landed in Auckland on my own. By God-incidence, my friend Janet was now living in Auckland and came to my rescue. There we were, like two old ducks at the airport, dragging my bags to the car. Knowing I would have to stay in Auckland for a while after my discharge, we had planned that I would stay with Janet and Derek until I was well enough to fly.

Before and after the procedures, Janet stayed with me. I remember lying on a trolly in the preoperative area with Janet standing by my side. When it was over, I awoke to see her sitting beside my bed. Given that I was not very hungry, she sacrificially ate my meals and snacked her way through my hospital stay.

The procedures were a success, and I was sent to rest and recuperate at Janet and Derek's home. It's a special thing to have a friend that you can stay with, all the while wearing a dressing gown and no makeup. Janet cooked for me, sat on the couch with me, and told me off for eating lollies in bed.

The time came to return home, and off I went with an appointment for a postoperative visit along with blood thinning medication and my usual antihypertensive drugs. I was so glad it was all over.

Once I was home, I expected my recovery would be akin to a miracle, but it wasn't. In fact, I was so tired that for the next few months I mostly just rested in my leather chair looking out the window towards the sea. My body had lived in a sort of battleground state for a long time, and I needed to recuperate. I listened to music, talked on the phone, prayed, and gave myself time to process the past year.

My emotions went up and down as I worked through the journey I had been on. We had spent thirty thousand dollars on the denervation and stenting, and I felt blessed to have been able to cover it. But there were also days when I felt sorry for myself and for the money I'd had to spend on my health over the years.

I returned to Auckland a couple of times to have my progress monitored. Disappointingly, the procedure didn't turn out to be the miracle I had hoped for. Still, it had made a difference, a big difference. The drugs were now more beneficial in controlling my blood pressure. I had been spared even more serious health issues by the discovery and subsequent stenting of my renal artery. And thankfully, I had no more hypertensive headaches, which, for me, was life changing.

―

At the start of the following year, we travelled to Hastings for the wedding of Janet and Derek's daughter. I'd had a warning in my spirit that going to Hastings might be a little ambitious and that my body still wasn't ready, but we went anyway.

In the end, it was an unforgettable day, and a wonderful weekend.

Heading back home, we stopped at a café just out of town for a coffee, where I collapsed and subsequently landed in Hastings Hospital for eleven days. I was so tired and worn out, and after the years of battle, my body just said stop. I could barely talk or walk, and after much testing but no definitive answers, I was told that I would recover but that I needed to go home and REST.

I did recover, but it took time. The upside of the weekend's incident was that my body was scanned from head to toe, which gave me a window into the toll that years of hypertension had taken on my body.

I remember watching the tidal flow from our lovely home in Aotea and seeing the float planes coming and going. It reminded me of the ebbs and flows of life. As I rested, I wondered how many multitudes of people there were like me who, for whatever reason, were confined to their home, unable to live what the world considered 'normal lives'.

I got my strength back, but I wasn't the same. My heart had changed. My values had changed. There was a time when it mattered to me what people thought, how they perceived my health, even what they made of the fact that I did or didn't work. It just didn't matter so much anymore. I learned to be happy, to have a new perspective about my life, even though it wasn't what I had planned. I had found a new peace.

- 24 -

Found

It had been a season of healing and recuperation, and I was ready for a new adventure to begin. Over a period of several months the name of a city in the South Island of New Zealand had repeatedly come to mind. The city was 'Nelson'. I completely ignored this as there was no way I was going to move to the South Island—not that I had a problem with the city of Nelson; in fact, I knew it to be a very desirable place to live. It was the thought of leaving my children and my friends, and moving to a place where I didn't know a soul. I put the whole situation down to my imagination and ignored it.

One day Geoff and I were having morning tea in a café and because I had sensed a restlessness in him, I asked him what his dreams were. To my shock, he shared something I had never heard him say before. He told me he wanted to live in Nelson. He wanted to enjoy the sunshine and go fishing and partake of all the outdoor activities Nelson was well known for.

Geoff had recently resigned his position as Deputy Principal of the secondary college and had taken early retirement. This was to be the first of five retirements. Each time he would retire, something else would beckon him into employment once more.

I am ashamed to admit that when Geoff shared his dream, I was not the supportive, loving wife that I would like to have been. I had a complete knee-jerk reaction and told Geoff there was no way I was going to leave my family and friends and move to Nelson.

So, we left the subject alone and didn't talk about it again for weeks. But during this time I was still hearing the word 'Nelson' in my mind. I just couldn't seem to get it out of my head.

One day I decided to have it out with God. I sat in my leather chair facing out to sea and asked something ridiculous. I prayed that if He really was sending us there to live, God would lead me to a verse in the Bible that would point us to Nelson.

Much to my surprise, I felt strongly to look up a particular section of the Bible called the Psalms. I opened my Bible to the Old Testament, and carefully read a Psalm, all the while trying to imagine how any verse could possibly include the word 'Nelson'. I soon came to the end of the particular Psalm I was reading, and to my utmost shock, I read the following words: *The Holy Bible, New King James Version, Copyright 1982 Thomas Nelson. All rights reserved.*

There it was! It seemed impossible. Never in my dreams did I imagine that contained within the Bible was the word, Nelson. Now to the more theologically dogmatic person I feel I may be met with criticism at my methods and requests of God, but I give Him permission to correct me if I am taking things too far.

Without a doubt, from that moment forward I knew we would be heading to Nelson. I didn't know when, but I knew it was coming. I kept this in my heart and waited.

Soon after that experience, Geoff attended a large farming agricultural fair with a friend. A few days later I received a phone call from a rather excited Geoff. In his enthusiasm to live in Nelson he had gone ahead and applied for a job there, however he had not been appointed. This was some months ago, just after he had told me he wanted to live there. Now he was calling to tell me he had just received a subsequent job offer for the position of Senior Advisor for the Ministry of Education, and it was in Nelson. Without hesitation I told him to accept it, as my heart had already been prepared.

I have noticed that once a season changes in our lives, things can happen with great speed. You feel like your life is one never-ending, repetitive routine, and then, *Bang!*, everything changes, and you feel as if you are running to catch up. That's how it has been in my experience, anyway.

Geoff was asked to take up his position in Nelson within three weeks of accepting the offer! We decided that he would go on ahead. I would stay back to sell the house and join him when all the details were sorted out. By this time, I was an old hand at moving house. I took on the whole process like an unpaid job, right down to working out transportation for the dog and cat.

Geoff, in turn, would commence house hunting in Nelson and settle into his new job. He would come back on weekends when it was possible. We expected our house to sell almost immediately, even though the housing market in our area was rather slow at the time. My thought was that if God was in this, then He would make it happen. Well, God was in this, and things happened, but not the way I had planned or predicted.

I remember praying a simple request at the time—that through the sale of our house, we would make the money back that I had used to pay for the surgery in Auckland. The housing market at the time meant it was more likely that we would only get what we had paid for the house (or slightly more), so it was a bit cheeky, but I asked God anyway.

I recall one particular buyer who kept making offers on our house. It was the same amount we had paid for the house and because I fully believed we were going to get more, we turned his offer down. He eventually raised his offer by five thousand dollars, but I still said no. Friends were telling me to take the money because at least we weren't selling at a loss, but I went with my gut feeling and again said no. He persisted for a number of months, even sending us a message through the estate agent telling us we would regret not accepting his offer. He was mistaken—turning down his offer was the right decision, and one we would definitely not come to regret.

∼

During this time, someone precious to me died. It was the mother of the family we had grown up living next door to. This family had treated our family as their own. 'Aunty Nessie' had lived into her nineties, and had been in a retirement village about an hour away. When we received news of her death, Geoff came home to attend the funeral with me.

Aunty Nessie's funeral is one of those days that will forever be etched into my memory. I remember I wore what I jokingly called my 'posh' coat with a fur collar, and even though it was a sad day, I was also looking forward to it because my childhood friend, Lynda, Aunty Nessie's daughter, was back from New York. I also realised that others might be there who I had not seen for a number of years.

The church was packed, and we were waiting for the funeral to commence when someone tapped me on the shoulder and informed me that a lady seated over to the right of us was trying to get my attention. Leaning forward, I looked to see who it was.

She was unmistakable with her copper red hair, and freckles that were still splashed all over her face like thousands of small stars lighting up a galaxy. Many years had passed. Surely it was only yesterday that we sat in the damp grass eating our sandwiches while she explained to me where babies come from.

Looking at each other with rows of chairs between us and people taking their seats, we both started to wave. It was Chrissy. I had found her at last! I could see at a distance that she was starting to cry, and we both just stared at each other laughing and crying at the same time.

I had searched every avenue I could think of on social media and had never found her. Yet as it turned out, all this time she was only an hour away. Chrissy was the charge nurse of the retirement village where Aunty Nessie had lived. I had even visited Aunty Nessie, yet never once had we crossed paths.

My family knew of my search, and as I rang them later that day, all I had to say was, "Guess who I have found?" and they all immediately said, "Chrissy." They knew who she was. Over the years I had talked about her many times. Now at last I had found her.

It was a beautiful farewell to Aunty Nessie. As soon as it was over, Chrissy and I made a bee line for one another. It was like the hug of two little girls running through the playground and connecting once more. Geoff politely ignored us as we held hands and walked to the room where the refreshments were being served.

We held on to each other almost as if we were scared to let go in case we lost each other again. We had so much to share! Chrissy had travelled the world, married Lee, the love of her life, and had three sons. Her career had been extensive. In truth, she had led the life that I had dreamed of.

As Chrissy talked, I began to think that maybe I should go and chat with others who had attended the funeral, but Chrissy seemed keen to just spend time together reconnecting. It was at this point I said a quiet internal prayer. It was more of a question. I wanted to talk to Chrissie, but I also felt I needed to reconnect with others who were there. It was at that moment the following words clearly came into my spirit: "She needs you."

I stood there having a quiet battle with God. I told Him He was wrong. Chrissy's life was amazing. She was all I ever aspired to be—she didn't need me at all. But I loved being with her, and so we just kept talking and, in the end, didn't circulate or meet others in the hall that day.

As we turned to leave, Chrissy told me she would contact me in a week or so to arrange a catch up. At this point she proceeded to tell me that in the past she had suffered from a good deal of shoulder pain which had resulted in surgery on her spine. She then informed me in a very casual way, almost as if she were telling me she had an ingrown toenail, that she had a tumour on her brain, but that she was fine. She had some dizziness and had begun dragging her foot but was having a biopsy that week to determine the size of the tumour and to see if her other symptoms might be related. She would contact me after the biopsy.

I was a little surprised, but accepted it was all in hand because she was so casual about it. But the truth was, Chrissy had a brain tumour, it was cancerous, and it was very serious indeed.

In hindsight, I came to understand that Chrissy was underplaying the whole situation. She talked very matter-of-factly about the biopsy, almost brushing it off as insignificant. In fact, she was so dismissive of her health situation that at the time I didn't fully take in what she was saying. I soon came to realise that Chrissy never dwelt on what she was going through but instead focused on others and their needs. She was a very special lady indeed.

That week Geoff returned to Nelson. I had told Chrissy we were selling up and going to live in the South Island. We both agreed it was bad timing—we had only just reconnected! I waited for her call with anticipation, but three weeks passed, and I heard nothing from her. I began to think that perhaps the excitement over meeting once more had been one-sided and that she had forgotten to ring me. I was disappointed but realised that many years had passed and that she had a busy life.

Then late in the third week, I received a phone call. It was Chrissy's husband. Chrissy had asked him to contact me. He told me that while she had undergone the biopsy there had been a medical mishap. Chrissy had had a stroke. She had been in Intensive Care, but her condition was improving and she was being transferred to a hospital just twelve minutes' drive from my house to begin the long road to recovery—recovery in that she was now going to have to learn how to live with being paralysed down one side of her body.

Hanging up the phone, I could literally hear my heart pumping over my thoughts. I sat down and tried to take it all in. Those words that day that she needed me were coming to pass but in a way that I couldn't have imagined. I was alone in my house waiting for it to be sold, Geoff was already situated in Nelson, and apart from preparations for moving, I had lots of free time. Now I understood. I would spend as much time as I could with someone that meant so much to me, Chrissy.

So it began. I would arrive at the hospital and sit with my childhood friend. She was struggling to deal with such a sudden loss of independence. But she was a fighter, and nothing was going to hold her back.

I talked with her about my journey, how I had discovered my faith, and who God was to me. She listened patiently but always finished with saying something like, "It may work for you, Janet, but it's just not for me."

We talked and laughed and downloaded to one another all our joys, our fears, and life's ups and downs. There were so many years to catch up on. Chrissy had a fire in her belly to get strong and nothing was going to stop her.

Finally our house sold. We didn't just get enough to make up for my surgery, as I had asked of God. We got almost three times the amount! In the market at the time, this was a fantastic offer, and we gratefully accepted.

Chrissy was soon strong enough to be discharged. She was going to her house, an hour up the coast to a beautiful seaside place called Kapiti. This was the very place we had lived after we sold our house on the hill, but I had never met up with her during that time. I was able to visit Chrissy in her home before I left for Nelson. We were sad to be parting ways. I imagined I wouldn't see her for a long time, but we agreed to catch up regularly on the phone.

Little did I know that Chrissy would become an even bigger part of my life in the near future.

～

We were blessed with a beautiful home in Nelson. Once again it had stunning sea views, and for over a year we enjoyed living in this wonderful place. It was a time of getting to know Geoff in a new way. We knew almost no one in Nelson, so Geoff and I became great friends, taking every opportunity to tour around the South Island of New Zealand.

Then one day about a year later, Geoff shared with me that he was missing our family and friends back home. He wondered if we should consider returning to Wellington. I understood why he was feeling this way. I had social media, and often caught up with friends and our children on the phone, but he didn't. As we prayed and talked about it, we felt the season was coming to an end. Geoff had lived in his dream town, and we had developed a strong friendship. It was time to go back.

Geoff applied for a position as manager of community ministries for the Salvation Army in Porirua and was successful. His new role would involve supervising a team of psychologists and financial capability trainers, running a food bank, and managing transitional housing. We sold our home for a profit and headed back again. Our time in Nelson had been wonderful, but it was over.

Returning to Wellington, we discovered a market with few houses for sale. We noticed, however, a house back in Kapiti, where we had previously lived. This was much further out of town than we had anticipated, but we loved the house, and even though it was way too big for us, we bought it.

Soon we had settled into Kapiti. Our new home was only a five-minute drive from Chrissy's house, and she and I soon began a routine of doing something together on Thursdays. Chrissy's husband would help her into my car. Chrissy couldn't walk far because of the paralysis, and she walked with a tripod-style walking stick, but this didn't stop us. We soon became familiar with all the cafés in our locality.

I remember driving my car on to the beach and right up to the sea. I realised this probably wasn't good for my car but didn't care as we sat with the tide splashing around the front wheels.

My son Cameron had been at a charity auction and bought me a framed drawing of a flower and underneath the flower the artist had written the word, Found. I gave this to Chrissy as a memento of finding her after all these years.

In time Chrissy's condition began to deteriorate to the point where she was wheelchair-bound. It was becoming more difficult to get her in and out of my car, and she had trouble speaking. I knew that at some point we would have to keep our visits to just having coffee at her house.

I knew Chrissy was dying and tried to share my faith, but she always told me it wasn't for her. One day, we were alone in her house. I knew I only had a small window of opportunity, and I also knew I had a captive audience because at that point Chrissy couldn't vocalise her thoughts properly and tell me to shut up.

I jumped in boots and all. I told her that God loved her very much and that somehow along life's journey she had mixed up religion with

God. I explained that religion is a vehicle that people use as an outlet of worship and spiritual growth, and that it's meant to be healthy and relational but that sometimes people (often with good intentions) have added traditions of their own that in fact have little to do with who God is. I shared that in a worst-case scenario, some aspects of religion have become damaging and controlling, that some religious communities had become quite the opposite of the original intention of the founders of the church.

I shared with Chrissy that Jesus Himself spoke against such people. They were like the Pharisees—strict observers of religious rites and traditions, but who put heavy burdens on people making it almost impossible to understand that God is Love and that His love is unconditional.

For they bind heavy burdens, hard to bear, and lay them on men's shoulders: but they themselves will not move them with one of their fingers.
Matthew 23v4

But woe to you, scribes and Pharisees, hypocrites! For you shut up the kingdom of heaven against men; for you neither go in yourselves, nor do you allow those who are entering to go in. Woe to you, scribes and Pharisees, hypocrites! For you devour widows' houses, and for a pretence make long prayers. Therefore you will receive greater condemnation. Woe to you, scribes and Pharisees, hypocrites! For you travel land and sea to win one proselyte, and when he is won, you make him twice as much a son of hell as yourselves.
Matthew 23v13-15

I didn't have time to share these scriptures with her but I tried to explain to Chrissy what the Bible said about Pharisees and how they had twisted the message of God, and that this continues even today in some parts of the wider church.

I told her that there were wonderful people who loved God in the churches, but that there were also those who for wrong reasons used religion to put people in invisible chains. I explained that the church in itself was good and there were some incredible places of worship out there, but sometimes the true message had got lost, and we needed to determine the difference. I told Chrissy that God was waiting for her with open arms and all she had to do was call out to Him from her heart and receive His love.

Of course, I cannot recall verbatim what I told her, as time has passed, but in summary this is what I think I said to her that day.

When I was finished, I wondered if anything I had said made sense. Chrissy's eyes were fixed on me. I looked at her and asked her if she had understood. She nodded her head and said yes. I was concerned I had made a mess of the message, but in the end I realised it was up to God to unjumble what I had tried to say.

I went home that day hoping I hadn't made a mess of things. I knew that she understood what the Bible said about God, Jesus Christ and the Holy Spirit being a trinity, the three in one. She knew the foundational truths of Christianity but as far as I could understand had seen the adverse effects of religion in the world and rejected God due to that. Apart from that she never went into too much depth with me except to repeatedly tell me that she was glad my faith worked for me, but it didn't for her.

Soon, Chrissy was moved into a hospice. One day I arrived, and it was clear the family was gathering. Family had come from different parts of New Zealand and even Australia. I walked into the family room where visitors could have something to drink and sit for a while. I saw familiar faces from my childhood. To me they all looked the same as they did all those years ago, but I guess in reality that was impossible. Some recognised me, but others, who were in highchairs when I used to stay at Chrissy's house, clearly didn't.

We stood around chatting, but in my heart I was just wanting a short time alone with Chrissy. Then out of the blue Lee appeared and said to me, "You've got five minutes alone with her Janet."

Well, I didn't need any encouragement. I almost ran to her room. On entering I saw a bed, and in it, covered in warm bedding, was Chrissy. The only part showing was her head, and she lay on her side facing the window.

I sat at the side of her bed and put my face close to hers. "Chrissy, it's Janet here," I said. She opened her eyes and half nodded her head in acknowledgement of me. "Chrissy," I repeated, "can you hear me?" She made it clear she could.

Then I said, "Chrissy, have you called out to Jesus?"

Looking at me, Chrissy clearly and deliberately said, "Yes."

I knew our time together was short, so I then said, "Chrissy, I want to ask you something. When I come to heaven—and I will come when it's my time—will you be there to meet me?"

Once again, she looked straight at me and she said, "Yes I will." Then she drifted off to sleep once more. I kissed her forehead and said goodbye. I was going to see my treasured friend again, and I knew it without a shadow of a doubt.

I walked out of the hospice that day thankful for my childhood friend.

Not too long after that, Chrissy was transferred to Seven Oaks, the very retirement home where she had been charge nurse. Sometime earlier, the staff there had made a blanket for her, full of embroidered mementos about how much she meant to them. She meant a lot to many people. The staff lovingly cared for her till she passed away.

I heard that when Chrissy's body was taken from the retirement home the staff lined either side of the road and formed a guard of honour for her all the way to the hearse.

Funnily enough, Chrissy's family name is Nelson. The word I had repeatedly heard in my heart had more than one meaning and indicated a special season in my life. Words are never lost on God, and nothing is coincidence.

Chrissy was a friend to many, a wonderful mother to her three boys, and the beloved wife of Lee. Hers was a life well lived.

Till we meet again.

- 25 -

Cliff Diving

It was a lovely spring day, and I had just been for a walk along the beach with the dog. Each day we followed a similar route—through the gate at the bottom of our garden, across the park, into a short street, then we would cross the road and enter a small windy track which led to the beach. Reaching the end of the track, we were greeted by the stunning view of Kapiti Island, just five kilometres across the sea from the beach.

Rain, hail or shine we would saunter along the foreshore, scattering seagulls everywhere. I always admired the ever-moving mounds of driftwood and seaweed that were strewn across the beach and sand dunes. Often there were fishermen to chat to or other dog owners. There was never time for boredom along this picturesque route.

It was just another day, but as I was leaving the beach, I became aware of a niggling feeling that had been with me for the past couple of weeks. It was a sense that change was coming, only I didn't know what it was.

On my way home I was talking to God about the uneasy feeling I had about whatever was on the horizon. Just as I came to cross the street, I sensed God speaking to my heart. It was just as if a man walked past and spoke to me as he walked by. It was clear and unmistakable: "Get your house ready for sale. You are on the move."

I stopped and stood still trying to take in what I had just heard.

Being that I am what some might call a serial mover, I didn't have an issue with selling our house. But we had tenants in one part of our home, and it was a huge house with a large garden and we had lots of furniture, so a move would involve a lot of culling and gardening.

Ever the optimist, I immediately thought something wonderfully exciting must be about to happen if it meant we had to move house.

So there I was, standing on the street with the dog and feeling a sense of happy anticipation about what I had just heard. I had no idea that something terrible was about to take place. There was a dark cloud on the horizon and it was coming our way, and if I was to be able to deal with it, selling the house would be almost a necessity. So that evening I talked to Geoff, and he agreed we would prepare to move.

I began to clear out our house. I took carload after carload of clutter and excess to the local second-hand shops. I gave things away and spent much of the next few weeks making my home look presentable for sale. I removed bags and bags of weeds and leaves. Everything was starting to look pristine. I was in my element, and I found the whole experience rather cathartic. Our lovely tenants had a change of situation and told us they were moving, which meant the apartment was about to become empty. Everything was going well.

Over the following days I started to pray and think about which real estate agent we would ask to sell our house. I had no idea where we were going, but that was fine. I knew what I had heard, and I was excited.

I also knew that our wonderful daughter Kimberley and her husband Aaron would let us live with them for a short time until we had a clear direction about the next step. They had been lumbered with us before, and I hoped they wouldn't mind if we arrived on their doorstep with the dog once again.

During this time, a man's name kept coming to mind, a bit like a thought that wouldn't go away. It was the name of a man I had met through my sister a couple of years before. I had met him once at a luncheon. He had such a magnetic personality and huge heart that the atmosphere in the room felt as if it had to expand just to hold his presence. I had asked my sister Anne about him at the time, and she explained to me that he and his wife had walked through incredibly difficult times and had seen miracles and outcomes that were birthed out of their total reliance and faith in God.

Ivan Wong Kee is one of those people who you only need to meet once, and you will remember him. Chatting with him over lunch that day, it had soon become apparent that this man's Christian faith didn't just stop at the door. It saturated every part of who he was and still is. He was also a real estate agent. I began to wonder if he would be the right person to sell our house for us.

I finally plucked up enough courage to contact Ivan. I wasn't brave enough to ring him in case he didn't remember me, so I took the easy road and messaged him on Facebook.

It wasn't long before I got a reply. He remembered me, but disappointingly said he was not able to sell real estate in our area but could recommend someone else. *Fair enough*, I thought. But for some reason, I never got around to contacting a local agent.

A couple of days later, I received a call from Ivan. He gave me the name of an agent who could list houses in our district, and if I was happy about it, Ivan would work with him to sell our house. I needed no convincing. I had felt such a sense that Ivan was the one to sell our house that I quickly agreed.

What I didn't know was that Ivan had made a pledge to God that he would give away the commission on his next few house sales to benefit the church and community. He was literally giving it all away. I felt humbled to even be part of what Ivan was doing. I soon came to understand that this man and his wife were a rare breed indeed. To them, money was just another tool to channel God's love and bring healing to people's lives, not just in New Zealand but in other parts of the world as well.

So we set a date for Ivan and another agent to view our home and provide an appraisal. I felt the date was perfect timing. Geoff would be away on his annual pilgrimage to the South Island where he would stay for five days in a beautiful place called the Marlborough Sounds. There he would fish and relax with friends and recharge his batteries.

Being in a fairly isolated area meant it was like a retreat from the outside world. I knew that if Geoff had been at home he would have had a lot to say to the agents, and we would quite likely have both been talking excitedly about the house at the same time. There was a good possibility that we would overwhelm the real estate agents, they would make a hasty retreat, and that would be the last we would see of them.

The day Ivan and his estate agent co-worker came to do the appraisal was such an enjoyable day. The fact that I love houses and God, meant I was in my element with Ivan, and we had a lot to talk about. When they left, I once more felt the excitement of change and wondered what lay ahead.

I was about to find out.

On Saturday the fifteenth of December, I continued to prepare our house for sale. Geoff was still in the South Island, and I was at home thinking about our friend Jeremy's birthday party, which I was to attend that evening.

I was sitting on the couch in the early afternoon with my laptop on my knee, just relaxing, when the phone rang. I got up to answer the phone, as I had left it on the other side of the lounge. Picking up the phone, I heard a voice I didn't recognise. It was the farmer who managed the land where Geoff was holidaying. That took me by surprise, but she sounded chirpy enough, so I presumed she was calling to pass on a message from Geoff. However, she proceeded to give me quite unexpected news—Geoff had fallen off some rocks, and although she was sure he would be fine, a rescue helicopter had been called and was currently transporting Geoff to Wellington Hospital.

Little did I know how much she had understated the situation in order to protect me from getting too much of a shock. Geoff had, in fact, fallen off a cliff, landing headfirst on the rocks about five metres below. His eventual hospital discharge notes would read:

Significant head laceration . . . C1 arch fracture, C2

transverse foramen fracture, C7 spinal process fracture. Left knee injury—complete and partial tears of ACL, PCL, MCL, MPFL, LCL. Damaged medial meniscus and associated surrounding soft tissue injuries.

In summary, he was a mess. He had a massive head wound, three neck fractures, and a leg that was facing in a very strange direction from the knee down.

But at this point in time, I didn't know any of that. I recall hanging up the phone and feeling a little spaced out. I didn't know what to do. I realised that Geoff's injuries must be serious because a rescue helicopter was involved, but my brain didn't seem to be firing correctly. I guess I was in some degree of shock after all.

Gathering my thoughts, I realised I needed to get to Wellington Hospital, a trip of about one hour and ten minutes. But first I would ring my children.

Kimberley, on hearing the news, insisted that she and Aaron drive to our house and pick me up. This was a good idea, as I don't think I could have concentrated safely on driving.

I rang Cameron and was surprised to hear that he was already in the car with our pastor. They were heading into Wellington to watch a movie. *Was it possible God was in the background organising things, and that for whatever reason, He wanted our pastor at the hospital as well?*

I then called the dog kennels to ask if they could take Belle for as long as needed. I didn't know when I would be back home and thinking about the dog was an extra worry I didn't need just then. I remember thinking that phoning the kennels was a bit of a waste of time because you usually have to leave a message and then wait for them to ring back. But this time, someone actually answered the phone, and kindly told me they would open the kennels outside of opening hours just for me to drop the dog off.

Realising that Geoff's helicopter could land on the landing pad on the hospital roof at any time and that we were still a long way from the hospital, I took a chance and rang my sister Anne. I remember asking her if she happened to be near Wellington Hospital. She was! She and Graeme were out for a drive, and it wouldn't take them long at all to get to the hospital. They would be at the hospital for Geoff when he arrived.

Kimberley and Aaron were nearly at my home by now. I should have started to prepare myself and perhaps pack an overnight bag and get the house ready to be locked up for a few days. But logical thinking seemed to elude me completely.

Instead, I rang our friend Jeremy and very calmly told him that I was sorry, but I could not attend his birthday party because Geoff had fallen on some rocks. Then I proceeded to empty the dishwasher. This was ridiculous, of course, because I needed to get ready, but my brain seemed to go in another direction, and I robotically stood there putting dishes away. It was at that moment I felt a deep sense of calm come over me. It literally stopped me in my tracks. I stood there with dishes in hand, and just knew it was all going to work out. Geoff would survive. Now I was able to gather myself and prepare to head into the hospital.

Once we were on the road, I called our church lifegroup leaders, who started the ball rolling and contacted people to pray for Geoff. Then I phoned my sister Caroline, who informed me that her husband, Dave, who is an airline pilot, had just landed a plane at Wellington Airport, and said she would contact him. Very soon, he arrived at the hospital as well. *Was this all just chance—all these people in the right place at the right time?* I don't think so.

On arrival at Wellington Hospital, we were escorted into a cubicle in Accident and Emergency. I had been here before—this was where I had seen my dad have a massive heart attack. I knew this cubicle was where the most seriously ill patients were taken to be assessed and given urgent medical attention.

Pulling aside the curtain and stepping into the area where Geoff was, I literally froze. My legs felt as if they might buckle beneath me. Staff were working on Geoff, but I could see that huge bandages were wrapped around his head, and his face was a bloodied pulp. His eyes were half closed and bulging. One of his legs appeared to be twisted in a way that didn't look normal. He wore a large plastic collar to keep his neck still. There was blood everywhere, on the floor and on the bed. My sister and her husband and other family members were there as well.

I went to say something, but my mouth wouldn't move properly. That didn't seem to matter though because Geoff was conscious and talking nonstop. He was either on drugs or full of adrenaline; his cheerfulness was completely at odds with the sight in front of me. At any rate, he seemed to be very thankful he was alive.

The sight of Geoff was all rather ghastly, and I needed a moment to take it all in. I backed my way out of the cubicle and took myself off to the family room. Kimberley came and sat with me, and a lovely Pacific Island lady kept smiling at me from her seat in the corner. I tried to smile back, but my brain seemed to be disconnected somehow from my face so I just sat staring at the wall. *Was Geoff going to die? Was he going to be able to walk again?* My mind was racing with worst-case scenarios. An hour beforehand I had felt such incredible peace, but now I had lost that confidence because Geoff looked so terrible.

After about ten minutes I was able to gather myself and return to the cubicle again. By this time, I felt a lot calmer and was able to take the situation in properly. In reality, the brain is an amazing thing because within minutes we were taking photos of Geoff's beaten-up face, and bizarrely, Geoff was cracking jokes and laughing.

But the doctors were not laughing. It soon became apparent that a neurologist and a plastic surgeon were trying to work out which injury to deal with first. Eventually they decided to transfer him to another hospital nearby where Geoff would undergo plastic surgery on the large laceration on his head.

Geoff was loaded into the ambulance and, knowing that I wouldn't be able to see him again until the next day, I decided to drive home. Various family members offered me a bed, but I wanted to be at home where I could take stock of everything and give people an update on Geoff's situation.

It was very late that night when I finally crawled into bed. I was exhausted. Early the following morning, I drove back to the hospital.

This was to become my routine until Geoff was well enough to be discharged. But that day wasn't yet. There would be a number of hurdles for Geoff to overcome before he could be home with me again.

~

I found Geoff sitting up in bed and rather high on pain medication. I recall sitting on a chair beside his bed as he regaled the wonders of famous cricketers and retold the numerous cricket games he had either watched or played in. He seemed to think it was all rather marvellous and exciting. After hours of listening, I zoned out and started checking messages on my phone. Geoff didn't find that at all rude and continued to talk so loudly I think the entire ward heard him sharing his pearls of wisdom.

Eventually a nurse came to talk to me. She informed me that they wouldn't give Geoff any more of that particular medication, as he was clearly off his rocker. This information didn't appear to put Geoff off though, and I could still hear him droning on as I left the ward to go home that day.

The following day when I arrived at the ward, I was taken aside by a staff member and told to expect that Geoff may have personality changes due to his head injury. She explained that he could have anger issues, and that I shouldn't be too surprised if we had challenges ahead regarding his mental state. Without any thought I blurted out that she was wrong and told her everything was going to be fine. Nevertheless, I was repeatedly warned during Geoff's hospital stay to be prepared for possible personality changes. Thankfully, Geoff was fine. His personality never changed, and he remained the calm, happy individual he had always been. Somehow, I always knew this would be the case and that God had guarded his brain as he hit the rocks that day.

After one particularly long day at the hospital I arrived home to find Geoff's four-wheel-drive truck, which had been driven back by his friends from the South Island, sitting at the end of our driveway.

I think that was the first time I cried. It was the realisation his truck was back, but he wasn't, and I suddenly felt very alone.

In time, Geoff was sent back to Wellington Hospital to undergo more treatment. He was still on intravenous antibiotics and had a large dressing on his head covering the many sutures in his skull. He wore a large neck brace, and a leg brace with mechanical joints had now been added to his wardrobe. He looked a bit like a zombie in a horror movie, but he was getting better, and we were all thankful.

One day not too long after Geoff's accident, I was sitting at my dining room table thinking about his job. Geoff had resigned from his role at the Salvation Army and his last day had been the day before he had left for his fishing trip. However, he was on annual leave when he had the accident. That's when I realised that Geoff was by all accounts still employed until the annual leave had run out. I talked to my family about this, and they all agreed that Geoff was not entitled to accident compensation payments, but I thought differently. I began to make enquiries.

Sure enough, God had taken care of us once again. Geoff was entitled to weekly compensation payments, and these came as an immense blessing during his recovery.

Finally, the day came when Geoff was to be discharged. He was still really unwell, and I had to assist him to do everything. When I wasn't showering him, dressing him, or preparing food for him, Geoff would sleep. He slept and slept and slept.

Thankfully, I wasn't working or I would have had to leave my job just to care for him. I was now an unpaid nurse at home. It didn't help that we had a massive ant infestation during this time. One day I awoke to find ants throughout all our kitchen cupboards, on our benches and floors, and even in the toilet cistern. The exterminator came, but meanwhile I spent days washing all the household surfaces and cupboards and trying to look after Geoff as well.

People came and went—district nurses, occupational therapists, and other medical professionals—and the days just blurred into one, but slowly I started to see improvement. We became great friends with the occupational therapist who was our most frequent visitor.

Slowly, Geoff started to look like himself again, but we still had a long way to go.

By this time I could see that the word I had received about moving house had been very timely. I knew I couldn't manage our large section and house alone. Ivan had already been around to do the appraisal—now it was time to sell our house.

So it was that Ivan and his colleague listed our home, and within approximately two weeks it sold for a price we were thrilled with. Everything was coming together. Before long we bought another house. This house wasn't in Kapiti, but in Aotea. We both felt we were to move closer to Wellington and that this home was meant for us. This too was for reasons that would soon become apparent, but meanwhile, we unpacked and began to enjoy our new home with its extensive sea views and friendly neighbours.

By the time we moved, Geoff had improved so much he was only wearing a scaled-down neck brace. He worked hard on getting his leg to function properly, and once again he beat dire predictions that he would struggle with mobility in the days to come. He walked and walked until his leg became strong.

Later that year, Geoff was getting dressed one morning when he felt a weakness and reduced sensation creeping down the left side of his body. It started in his hand, then moved down to his left leg. Recognising that Geoff was possibly having a stroke, I called an ambulance. Here we were, back in Accident and Emergency, but again, within a short space of time Geoff recovered. It appeared he had suffered from a minor, self-resolving type of stroke. The cause was unknown, but it was possibly the result of a blood clot from after his fall.

Much to Geoff's annoyance, his driver's license was suspended for a period of four weeks. This was the third occasion in our married life that his license had been suspended. The ultimate marriage test was now being repeated, as once more he assisted me with hand signals and what Geoff called 'helpful directions'.

It was a great relief when Geoff was permitted to drive again and his independence was restored. Once again, Geoff had been protected from a situation that could have been much worse. Throughout this entire journey we both had such a sense that God had this sorted, and that everything would work out okay, and it did.

In fact, Geoff's recovery was so miraculous that when we told people what had happened to him, we would sometimes get a look that implied we were exaggerating. I soon learned to be ready to show people a photo of him in the cubicle after being airlifted to Wellington. Then there would be no doubt we were telling the truth. I had to be careful though, because on occasion I saw the blood drain from people's faces and it would become apparent the person was almost fainting at the sight of Geoff's mangled-looking body.

About six months after the accident, Geoff and I were chatting and I told him I wanted to go back to work. Geoff hadn't worked since before the accident, and his compensation payments had now stopped. It wasn't that we were desperate for the money—it was more about me wanting the independence of a regular income.

We sat in the sunshine looking out to sea and prayed together. Well, I prayed, and he listened. I basically asked God to provide me with a job. Annoyingly, my prayer was interrupted by a phone call. Geoff's phone was ringing, and he wanted to answer it.

The call was from someone at the local community college, offering Geoff a tutoring job. He hadn't even applied for a position there!

Geoff hung up the phone and we laughed and laughed. God had moved a mountain, but not the one I wanted. It was a job for Geoff, not me. Geoff had progressed so much since the accident that he felt quite able to accept the position, so he did. I recall being a bit annoyed and overlooked at the time. What I didn't know was that I was heading towards another surgery, or that the situation in our wider family was about to change and my heart wouldn't be in a job, but in something entirely different.

Life is full of curveballs, unexpected moments, and often challenging situations. Geoff's scars are barely visible now, and although there are momentary reminders of this time, such as tiredness, it's hard to imagine he was as sick as he was. I still have the photo on my phone to prove to people how far he has come, and I have to remind Geoff when he climbs ladders or takes risks, that he has had serious injuries and is not superman.

The first time Geoff went back on his annual fishing trip to the Marlborough Sounds, I was half expecting another call to tell me something else had gone wrong, but all was quiet. To this day he continues to take his fishing trips and I continue to pray for his safe return. I guess life's like that—you have to look past the risks and keep enjoying the adventures. I've also accepted that once a fisherman, always a fisherman, and I still look forward to eating the catch when he comes home.

- 26 -

Anchored

Following Geoff's accident and subsequent selling of our home, we had moved to a house with lovely sea views. I guess with every blessing you get a downside. In this case, with the views came the wind. The downside of the wind was that we often couldn't relax outside because we might take flight. Some days I would rise in the morning to discover my large outdoor furniture lying upturned in bushes about thirty feet away. At night, we would often be asleep in our upstairs bedroom and the wind would shake the floor to the point that I would have to go and sleep downstairs. Our house was probably situated in the worst place for wind in the cul-de-sac. But it was a low maintenance home with a stunning outlook, and we were happy.

By now, Geoff had been tutoring for much of the previous year, and I was on the waiting list for what was hopefully going to be my last sinus surgery—an operation to improve the drainage from my frontal sinus and enlarge the opening of my nasal passage. I was still getting constant infections which left me feeling like I had a low-level flu most of the time. Yet we felt blessed about many things in our life, especially Geoff's miraculous recovery from his cliff-diving episode.

We retained close ties with our Kapiti friends. Geoff enjoyed our fortnightly life group so much that he insisted we travel almost an hour and a half each way to attend. Cruising up the coast to life group, we would stop at a restaurant near the beach for a meal on the way. The life group was held on a farm owned by a couple, Jeanette and Craig Irons. They were always so obliging and accommodating, and we developed relationships with a wonderful group of people as we enjoyed feasts and barbecues at their stunning home overlooking rolling hills and beautiful farmland. Their oversized fireplace would be lit, filling the room with a wonderful aroma and warmth. Life was good and we were looking forward to whatever lay ahead.

One morning toward the end of our first year in the house, my sister Anne and I met at the shopping mall for her birthday to have a drink and do some shopping together. I gave her a handbag I had purchased online. I was a bit embarrassed—it had looked so beautiful in the photo, but when it arrived it was more like a brick that had been painted in glossy blue paint. She said it was lovely but in truth I think she was just being kind, and somehow I couldn't imagine her parading around with this shiny blue box hanging off her shoulder.

I cannot say that Anne and I were two peas in a pod because that would be a lie. At times I've looked at siblings and thought how similar they are; they even walk and talk the same. That is not the case with me and my two sisters. All three of us are very different, and yet we are all the same in that we have all embraced the faith of our parents—a simple, uncomplicated Christian faith and the knowledge that God loves us all unconditionally.

When morning tea was over, Anne and I decided to take a walk around the mall. But as soon as we went to stand up, Anne sat back down. I thought this was strange and sat down too. That's when she told me a situation had developed over the past weeks—whenever she stood up, she got an unpleasant sensation in her head, as if it was 'full'. She assured me she had seen the doctor who had ordered some tests and she would be fine. I wanted to believe her, and tried to ignore the feeling that something was wrong with Anne's health.

In the end, we decided to give the shopping a miss, and headed off home. Anne put her shiny blue brick in the back of the car and hopped into the driver's seat. She told me she would sit for a minute until her head cleared. We said our goodbyes and I walked to my car and drove home.

My house was about twenty-five minutes away. All the way home I kept thinking about Anne and the strange sensation in her head. I thought I'd better check she had made it safely home, so as soon as I pulled into my driveway, I gave her a call only to find she was still sitting in the car park waiting for the feeling of pressure in her head to disappear. She had been sitting there for nearly half an hour! The pressure eased off shortly after this, and she finally made her way home, but I was concerned. Anne had always been physically strong. Her immune system seemed to fend off most bugs very easily. In fact, I often envied her strength and ability to do so much on any given day.

Following our conversation at the mall I tried to push away the feeling that something was seriously wrong. Anne was one of those people who appeared to be in command of any given situation, and I couldn't imagine her being seriously ill. I talked to my other sister Caroline about my concerns, but we knew Anne was seeking medical advice so we didn't think there was much we could do.

Soon after, my brother-in-law Dave flew into Wellington and was staying overnight. Caroline had flown up to meet him, and we decided to spend Friday evening together, along with Anne and Graeme.

Caroline and I were already at the restaurant with our husbands when Anne and Graeme arrived. The restaurant we had chosen was a colourful, Vietnamese diner with a large welcoming doorway. We watched as Anne held onto the door surround to steady herself as she stepped inside. Anne had undergone a knee replacement earlier that year, so she was still limping somewhat. But that night it was as if the limp had increased to the point that it appeared her legs were taking on a life of their own.

Anne made light of the situation, but once again I felt deep concern about something that yet had no name. But she was my big sister and she seemed to have the situation under control so everything must be fine, it had to be.

But all was not well. Not only was I concerned about Anne, but my daughter Kimberley had been admitted to hospital and required surgery. The operation was going to be at a private hospital in Wellington. It was scheduled for early in the following year.

―

Christmas came and went, and summer was whispering its goodbyes.

Early in the new year, my niece Melinda called in to our house. She mentioned that Anne had had a scan and had been asked to come into hospital the next day for a follow-up appointment.

The following morning, I was taking Kimberley to her specialist appointment. I knew we would have to drive past Wellington Hospital on our way home so I suggested that I would like to be in the outpatients waiting room when Anne arrived for her appointment. Anne could send me packing if she liked, but I would take the risk.

So there we sat, like a couple of highwaymen, ready to ambush Anne. When Anne appeared, she immediately saw us sitting there. Thankfully, she was delighted, and I mumbled something that made no sense, such as, I was nearby with Kimberley and thought we would call in.

Anne told me she was pleased to see me because two heads were better than one, and hopefully I would remember anything the specialist said if she didn't.

Before long, a nurse came and asked us to follow her. Kimberley remained in the waiting room, and I trotted along beside Anne.

As we entered a hallway off the waiting room, I looked up to see a sign on the wall. The words *Oncology Department* were written on the sign, and I felt my stomach sink. I looked at Anne, but she didn't seem to register what the sign had said. Perhaps God was protecting her heart in that moment.

We entered a small room with a bed, a desk, and two chairs facing the desk. A lady with a very kind face and equally kind manner came in and sat down behind the desk. Anne sat in the chair next to the specialist, and I sat in the remaining chair, facing directly towards Anne.

The lady introduced herself as the head of the oncology

department. Anne smiled at her and waited. I still saw no recognition on Anne's face that a bomb was about to drop or that her life was about to change forever.

I knew I had to be calm. This wasn't about me—I was needed in a support capacity, not as a blubbering, emotional wreck. Thankfully, I felt something encapsulating my emotions and keeping me calm in that moment.

The specialist looked at Anne's notes and appeared to be trying to find the right words. Looking over at me a couple of times, she mouthed the words, "Thank you for being here." That unnerved me because it made me feel what she was about to say was worse than I had imagined.

Then very calmly she looked at Anne and shared with her that the diagnosis was not a positive one. Anne had brain cancer, and she only had about three months to live.

I looked at Anne, and her eyes appeared to have glazed over. It was as if her brain was not registering what she was being told. She then looked at me and asked me if I had known this. I told her I knew she was not well, but I hadn't known what was wrong.

Then Anne started to cry—not a 'poor old me' cry, but a soft cry that sounded to me like the cry of someone who was resting her head on the shoulders of her beloved Jesus and weeping with Him. It was normal to cry, but there was something deeper here. It was as if God was sharing this moment with her and holding her in His comforting arms.

Then Anne spoke. She looked at the specialist and through her tears all she said was, "But my daughter is having a baby."

I felt so bad. Anne had grandchildren she adored, and they adored her. I had none at the time. *Why her and not me?* But life and death are not like that. It all seemed so unfair at that moment.

What we hadn't counted on, however, was the rousing of a mighty army that was about to take place as people from many places of worship and walks of life joined together to pray for Anne and contend for her life. The moment the call went out, it was like a trumpet blast as hundreds rallied to stand in the gap for Anne, supporting her and carrying her through the months to come, sometimes even in the wee small hours of the night.

Anne lived to see the birth of her grandchild. She defied the three months she had been given, and lived for another year and a half. In the months that followed her diagnosis, Anne touched many people's lives with her fortitude and inner strength. She soon lost her ability to walk, but that did not stop her from getting out and about, giving a listening ear, and making a positive difference wherever she went.

I've heard it spoken of people that they are going to be world-changers, that they will go places in life. I think that for many this means being spectacular on some level, getting up on a stage, or having a huge career. But it also means changing the immediate world around us. That's what Anne did—despite her physical brokenness she always asked how others were feeling or was happy just to listen to those who needed to know that someone cared. In that respect, she was a world-changer, in that she changed the world around her for good.

So here we were in this small room at the hospital, trying to take everything in. At this point Kimberley joined us, as she knew by the length of time we had been with the specialist that something unforeseen was going on. I phoned Graeme so he could come and be with Anne.

Anne's treatment began that day. A room had already been prepared for her so she could have some intravenous medication. It was all rather surreal. No one knew how to behave or what to say. I remember there was another man in the room also receiving intravenous medication. I felt sorry for him as he clearly realised that Anne had only just received her diagnosis. I saw him looking at the ceiling rather than looking our way. I could tell by the expression on his face that he felt as if he was intruding in a private family moment and he couldn't escape the room.

That day marked the beginning of a new journey for our family. Anne's beautiful children, David and Abbey, Nicola and Josh, and Melinda and Beau, and all the grandchildren would have many difficult and also special times as they supported their mum through the months that lay ahead.

I watched my brother-in-law Graeme work through many emotions in the days to come. I saw a man who hung on to his faith in spite of all the tumult that was going on in his life, a man of unwavering faithfulness to my sister, a man who cared for her and loved her in spite of some of the unpleasantness that having cancer would bring.

But I was about to go on a journey of my own, and it was a road on which I didn't particularly want to travel. For some people, family includes many cousins, aunts and uncles, and covers a multitude of people. But our family in New Zealand consisted of a small unit—our parents and their three daughters. We actually have a huge family, but they are in Holland and we grew up on the other side of the world. Although we three sisters were all married and had children, our childhood consisted of only five family members.

My parents were dead, and now my sister had cancer. If Anne left us, there would only be two of the original family left, Caroline and me. It was a strange and unwanted feeling, and it made me very sad.

Consequently, after Anne's diagnosis, I began to struggle. I held it together at the hospital, but alone at home I was a mess. I felt guilty for feeling this way as her family was going through so much more, but this only made me feel even worse. Whenever Anne would ring me, I chatted, laughed, and tried to be positive, but on my own I was struggling to hold it together.

From Tuesday to Friday after Anne's diagnosis I couldn't seem to stop crying. There were so many emotions all tied together. *Why her and not me? What about her children? What about Graeme?* On and on it went. I felt lost in a life raft on a wild and unpredictable ocean. I was annoyed at myself and the fact that I couldn't seem to stop the tears. I wanted to visit Anne, but I didn't want her to see me this way and I didn't know how to pull myself together.

On Saturday morning I woke up at around 5 a.m. Something had disturbed me but I didn't know what. Then out of the corner of my eye I saw movement off to my right. Now those who have had visions or spiritual encounters in life may concur with what I am saying.

Instead of thinking, oh gosh this is weird and I'm feeling scared, I felt very calm, and a deep peace came over me.

To my right as I lay in our bed, I saw Anne walk into the bedroom. Of course, Anne was not in our bedroom—she was tucked up at home in her own bed—so I was clearly having a vision of sorts. I followed her with my eyes as she walked around the bed and came and stood at the head of the bed next to me.

I turned and looked up at her. At that point, she looked down at me. How can I describe her face? It was completely beautiful. She was smiling, and it was a smile that seemed to spread across her entire face. I had never seen her so happy. Then she leaned over to speak to me. "Janet," she said, "I am going to be given a title."

No one explained it to me but I instinctively knew she meant a title such as a dame or a knight, a title we call a Queen's Honour. I looked at her and didn't say anything but my inner reaction to that statement was that Christians are not usually honoured for much of anything in this world, so whatever did she mean?

Instantly to my right came a voice. It seemed to come from the ceiling, yet it had no real point of origin. It was everywhere, yet nowhere. Anne was on my left, but the voice came from the right. It was as soft as a whisper, yet louder than a thousand trumpets. It was the most beautiful voice I had ever heard. The magnificence of this voice shook the atmosphere in the bedroom. It was the voice of the Holy Spirit, and He was speaking in reply to my thoughts:

> *"It is not a title; it is a crown. It is not earthly; it is eternal, and it is for services to the Body of Christ."*

At that moment I felt the power behind these words. I also felt the greatness of Anne's worth in God. I turned back to look at Anne, but she was gone. I knew what those words meant. According to the Bible, the Body of Christ refers to God's people. On earth we have only poor reflections of what is to come in heaven, such as titles and royalty. In heaven we are all royal daughters and sons of God, the King; we belong to a royal priesthood of believers. Anne had given much of her life to faithfully serving God and people, and she was going to be honoured for the way she lived her life, not on earth but in heaven.

This moment was so powerful and real and life-changing that instantly my excessive weeping stopped. Instead, I felt strength to cope with what was to come. Of course, there was natural grief, but the constant sadness and tears ceased.

It also made me realise that what we do for others on earth is not lost on God. Those who toil and feel they are invisible, are not. Everything we go through counts. Great or small, it all counts to God, and His love is beyond our limited understanding. Don't think that because you are not doing what Anne did with her life, you are not worthy of a crown, or that your life has counted for nothing. The Bible clearly talks about a crown of righteousness that is given to *all* people who hand their lives over to God.

But each of us is called to something different, and Anne's calling was a life of service to others. She did this faithfully—not perfectly, but faithfully. Each of us is called to different things. There will be no reward for doing something you are not called to do. Just be available, and God will show you the way.

So it was that I now could be the sister Anne needed, not the blubbering, useless kind. Part of me wanted to run over to her house every day, and I guess in truth becoming a pain to my brother-in-law. But I knew that I needed to be a sister, not a mother or a nurse. So I began a routine of visiting her one day a week, sometimes more, and just sitting and talking and being there.

Not too long after Anne's diagnosis she was admitted to hospital where it was decided she required a shunt to help drain the cerebrospinal fluid from her brain. She was booked for surgery the following week.

Meanwhile, I received a call from Wellington Hospital notifying me that my surgery had been moved forward to the following Tuesday. Kimberley was also booked in for her operation at the nearby private hospital on the following Wednesday. All three of us were having surgery the same week, and Anne and I were to be patients in the same ward! As it turned out, I never got to see Anne when I was a patient because I was too unwell and so was Anne, but it was one of those things that was so strange it was almost unbelievable.

When I was discharged after surgery, Geoff came and helped me gather my things to leave. From there we would make our way to the reception area of the hospital where he would leave me while he got the car and brought it to the pickup area in front of the hospital.

We got to the doors of the ward and saw another patient also being discharged, about to go through the same set of doors. It was Anne in her wheelchair, and Graeme was pushing her! We were being discharged at exactly the same time! We were even trying to get through the same set of doors at that same moment. If Anne or I had felt well, I think we would have found it the funniest thing ever. It really was so uncanny.

So there we were, Anne and me, sitting in the reception area of the hospital waiting for Geoff and Graeme to each get their cars. I was aware my hair looked like a bird's nest, and my face wore a large bandage across the nose. I was in old track pants and looked rather like a destitute person. Anne didn't fare any better—she had no hair and a large scar up the side of her head and was in her wheelchair. I looked at Anne and told her that I wouldn't blame our husbands if instead of returning to their less than glamorous wives, they had hopped in their cars and left town and were never coming back!

Thankfully they did return, and Anne and I parted ways for a few weeks. I knew that once I had recovered I could spend time with her, but I needed to get strong first.

So began a new routine. Graeme was able to work from home and carers came to assist with Anne's care. Graeme and Anne kept their home open for visitors, and many came and went over the months that followed.

∽

Around the corner from our house a lady lived whom I'd grown up with at the Salvation Army. There is a saying that others won't remember what you said and they will forget what you did, but people will never forget how you made them feel. This lady was a perfect example of such a statement.

When I grew up we were a family of three sisters at our church. There was also another family of two sisters and we were all similar in age. Then years later we found ourselves at the same church once again, except for my younger sister who lived in Christchurch. At this point we all had young children and we were very busy raising our families. By now you will understand that much of my life was one of being sick then getting better and then trying to catch up on missed days. As soon as I got on top of things, the whole business would repeat once more. In truth I was barely holding on, but I kept going because I truly believed that God was going to heal me and life was going to get better.

So here we were at the same church once more as the two sisters I had grown up with. I understood that they had walked a difficult journey in that they lost their dad when they were quite young. In fact, his was the first funeral I ever attended. Cancer had been in their life's experience, and I think that this had taught them to have great empathy for others.

It was during this season when our children were young that I had surgery. It wasn't an earth-shattering surgery or a life-saving surgery, but I remember being really sick for weeks afterwards. I have learned that when I have a general anaesthetic, I often feel emotionally quite low a few days after surgery. I think when the drugs are filtering out of your system your body is dealing with a lot. I've learned to expect this and yet the tears always come, and although I try to remind myself the feelings will pass, it doesn't help much at the time.

I was recovering from this particular surgery when the phone rang. I am telling you this as a reminder that special moments of thoughtfulness do count, and the recipients of those moments generally will remember. On the other end of the phone I heard the voice of one of the sisters I had grown up with. She was calling to ask how I was feeling after the surgery. That was it, my only phone call and it was her. I hung up the phone and felt like crying. The phone call was short and I suppose to some insignificant, but to me it was everything.

She may well have forgotten that moment, but I never have. Eventually we moved out of town and I didn't see much of her anymore. But I never forgot her kindness. This lady, Lynda Ford, may have been blessed with a natural beauty, but to me that one kind deed was the really special thing about her.

From that time forward I started to ask God, from time to time, that one day we could be more than just people mixing in the same social circles, that we could be friends. He was going to answer that prayer but it would be years until it happened, and it would become part of my journey with Anne.

Due to the fact we now lived in close proximity to one another, we had reconnected. When Anne was diagnosed with cancer, Lynda started to accompany me once a month to visit her.

I began to look forward to our outings as we made our way to Anne's apartment. We would always visit a café by the sea in a popular area called Oriental Parade. Lynda was delightful to be around—one of those people who isn't dragged down by all the negative events which seemed to bombard us on every news bulletin. Although the reason for our visit to Wellington wasn't a happy one, she lifted the atmosphere with her light-hearted banter. Most of all I never heard her speak ill of anyone. I enjoyed her company and was thankful she came with me once a month to visit Anne.

Graeme and Anne never turned anyone away, and visitors came day and night. I began to understand that although visitors were there to uplift Anne, they in turn would leave encouraged and strengthened and transfused with the grace to deal with situations in their own lives.

Lynda, Anne and I shared a common history, and we would recount past events and laugh till the tears ran down our faces. Our Fridays together became a special time as we all enjoyed each other's company.

The new year arrived, and it came with an unwanted gift. Menacing clouds were gathering, and these clouds were going to overshadow every country in the world with their darkness. The angel of death was about to pass over many lands, and millions were going to lose their lives. A pandemic was about to manifest itself, and the world was not prepared to deal with it.

As Covid-19 began to spread, one country after another went into a state of lockdown. Planes which once filled the air sat languishing at airports, businesses failed, faces were hidden behind masks, and hospitals were unable to cope with the effects of this virus. It was like a giant octopus with its tentacles reaching across the entire world.

Fear gripped the nations. As the media became awash with every shocking story that could be retold, fear itself became as terrible as the virus. Many caught the virus and literally had no symptoms at all, yet in some nations the devastation was so great that people were buried in mass, communal and hurriedly dug graves. There were other countries that remained relatively untouched in comparison.

Accusations were rife between various leaders of nations as to who was to blame. Conspiracy theories abounded, and in the end it became difficult to discern truth from fiction. In summary, the world was a mess.

During this time, New Zealand went into a very strict form of lockdown. For those who need the stimulation of people around them this was difficult. But for others it was a well-needed respite from the constant busyness of life. Anne was admitted to hospital over this time, and due to the restrictions of Covid-19, no one except Graeme could visit her.

For Geoff, lockdown was a time of suffering through his wife's experimental cooking and invented recipes and he bravely soldiered on through this difficult season. Each day another dish would be laid out before him, filled with weird and wonderful ingredients. The glazed look in his eyes told of a man who spent his days wistfully daydreaming about Indian takeaways and the taste of restaurant delights.

It was during this time of lockdown that a long-time friend, Judy Neeve, died of cancer. Though we were only streets away, we could only watch from afar as Jeremy, Judy's husband, and his adult children lovingly cared for her at home. Although Judy questioned many aspects of religion, she had an unswerving faith in God and she knew His peace and comfort. Jeremy told us later that she looked at him one day and with absolute conviction she said, "It is well with my soul." This total peace can only come from the heart of God as He prepared her to take her home.

Judy's funeral was held online due to the Covid-19 lockdown. We had all emailed photos of ourselves to the funeral director, and it was a moving sight to see our faces printed on A4-size paper and attached to each chair. As we all sat in our homes saying our farewells to Judy, her family lovingly performed a beautiful farewell service.

Finally we were allowed to go about our daily lives again, albeit with changes such as masks on public transport and social distancing where possible. While much of the world stayed in various forms of lockdown for many months, in New Zealand we were free to live relatively normal lives.

Each week I would see Anne deteriorate and yet maintain her brave outlook. She took each new challenge in her stride, mentally that is, because she had now been unable to use her legs for some time. She never lost her sense of humour, and at times would add her perspective about something that would send me into fits of laughter.

Anne had now been sick for such a long time that it was difficult to believe she was not going to survive this battle. There was always hope for another miracle and although there were many along the way, her physical healing wasn't one of them.

It was a Monday morning in December when I received a phone call from my brother-in-law Graeme. He told me that Anne had taken a turn for the worse and he felt it was time to come and say our goodbyes.

We arrived at the apartment and the family began gathering. Anne lay in a hospital bed in the lounge. She wasn't conscious. She remained like this throughout the morning and into the early afternoon. At some point in the afternoon almost everyone decided to go for a walk and get some fresh air. Our son, Cameron, and Anne and Graeme's son, David, remained behind on a couch, chatting.

Apart from that, Graeme and I were alone with Anne. I was walking across the lounge when Graeme called me over. He had noticed a change in Anne's breathing. Not sure what to do, I grabbed Anne's left hand and Graeme held her right hand as gently and peacefully Anne slipped into the arms of her precious Jesus. She had loved and served God her entire life and now beyond a shadow of a doubt I knew that she was with Him.

The family were soon all back in the apartment, and with tears rolling down our faces, we laughed and cried and shared this unwanted, yet in many ways very special, moment.

Soon the pastor from Anne's church arrived, and some of her close friends. It was a strange yet weirdly normal situation. Anne had departed, yet her body was still in the room and family and friends were all around her.

The funeral director came and spent time preparing her body to be taken to the funeral home. When it came time to leave, he turned to me and shared that he had never before experienced an atmosphere such as this with a recently deceased person. He was right—not that I was familiar with dealing with death every day, but I felt what he felt, and it was special. I can only describe it as joy in the midst of sadness, and the sense of life over death in that room.

The funeral director arranged for the hearse to be driven to the basement carpark. Anne would be taken down by lift to be placed in the hearse. At this point Graeme and I both called out that we would be going down the stairs to meet the funeral director in the carpark. Then others followed, and it became a veritable stampede of about twenty people heading down the stairs leading to the basement.

The funeral director looked rather surprised at the mob that now appeared in the carpark but he was respectful of the moment. We all watched and prayed and said goodbye as Anne's body was gently placed in the hearse.

Seeing her there, I felt a tug in my heart. I wasn't ready to let go. I was going to escort the hearse up the levels of the carpark until it got to the exit doors and was able to merge onto the street. So, I ran to the front of the hearse and Graeme joined me, and we walked ahead of the hearse until it was time to say goodbye.

As the exit door opened, I ran out onto the road, then stepped back. As the hearse disappeared, Graeme and I walked, almost without speaking, back to the lift to the apartment.

Christmas was very close and people were already heading out of town for their annual festivities, so it was decided that Anne's funeral would be held just two days later. It was a sad day and yet a resounding joy filtered through everything. Anne was honoured by many, and deservingly so. Yet I knew in my heart that it was nothing compared to the joy that was now hers in heaven.

In spite of her situation, Anne had a peace that was evident to anyone who spent time with her in her final days. I've seen this peace and strength in other people, but I've seen it at its greatest in my loved ones who were not long for this world. I saw it and felt it in and around Anne, Judy, Oma, Opa, Chrissy, my sister-in-law Wendy, and others who have gone on before me.

Have you opened your life to God, or do you keep Him at a distance, disconnected to your heart and life? My story is not over, and without a doubt I know there are difficult days ahead and wonderful times that are also going to be mine. The name of this chapter, Anchored, was a reference to Anne, who was so clearly anchored to God. When the billows of life assailed her she wasn't shipwrecked because her hope was secured by the anchor of His love.

Seasons come and go. No sooner than we think we have it all together, a situation will come along and we realise we don't have it together at all. I watched my sister Anne lose so much physically. Bit by bit she was emptied of her strength, yet she had everything we all long for—a peace that passes human understanding. Her value was not attached to her failing body; it was in her faith in God and the knowledge that although her body would soon fail, her life was not over. She didn't sit preaching or spouting empty words; she just sat quietly, and her peace was evident to all.

Thank you, Anne, for anchoring me. Thank you for letting me share a little of your story. I know my loud laughter and excessive chatter drove you to distraction at times. That's what siblings do—they stretch each other by their differences and yet they love each other deeply.

My story will change and so will yours. People will come and go, jobs you had will become distant memories, churches will rise and fall, famous faces will become yesterday's news. Life moves on. But there are two things that will never change: God's great love for you; and the words of this Māori proverb:

> He aha te mea nui o te ao?
> *What is the most important thing in the world?*
>
> He tāngata, he tāngata, he tāngata!
> *It is the people, it is the people, it is the people!*

Acknowledgements

To my family. Geoff, you have stood by me unswervingly, never complaining, always supporting and encouraging me, even through the darkest of times. Cameron and Kimberley, you are cut from the same cloth as your dad. You always cheer me on from the sidelines and give me strength when I feel I have none left. Aaron, you are a gift from God, coming into a family like ours that all talk at once, pray randomly anywhere and anytime, and laugh uproariously at ourselves and each other. Thank you for being the perfect partner for Kimberley. I love you all and count myself blessed that you are the people God gave me as my family.

To my encouragers. Thank you to those who encouraged me to write this book. Sometimes I appeared to ignore your words because the thought of writing a book seemed too overwhelming. But in my heart, I was listening and taking on board what you said. It was your persistence that finally gave me the push I needed to write. So to Jeanette Irons, Stacey Nikora, Kathy Hardwick, and Michelle Miller: Thank you.

To the following extraordinary women. I've heard it said that to find a true friend is more valuable than gold. Well if that is the case, I am a rich woman indeed. You have been my armour-bearers and my encouragers. On some occasions you sat me down and gave me a hard word when I needed it, but you have also picked me up when I was feeling down. I am blessed with a number of treasured friends, but on this occasion I want to express my love and gratitude to Janet Lister, Vivienne Hill, and Mel McKenzie. I hope that if ever you need it, I can be there for you as you have been there for me.

To my wider family. To all my nieces, nephews and their spouses, my two sisters and sister-in-law (Anne and Wendy now in heaven) and my brothers-in-law. There are too many to name as the family keeps expanding, but I want to thank you. I love you all so much and thank you for just accepting me and abiding with the so-called 'crazy aunt'. Once again I count myself blessed that you are my family. You are all very special to me.

To Almighty God. It seems rather futile to try and capture words and then put them on paper to express my gratitude. You are eternal, almighty, and all-powerful, yet most of all you are inexpressible Love. This is all such a mystery to me, as often I haven't been the most loving of your children and yet you still love me. Thank you for carrying me when I have felt at times that I couldn't go on. I am glad this life of mine is only the beginning of an eternal relationship, and until my day comes and I see you face to face, I trust You to continue to hold my hand and walk with me through the ups and downs of life.

Finally, to so many people who have been with me throughout the different seasons of my life. I could never mention all of you by name. I appreciate each and every one of you, and although I can't thank you all in person, just know that I am ever so grateful for knowing you. I feel privileged that you have shared part of your life with me.

www.ingramcontent.com/pod-product-compliance
Lightning Source LLC
Chambersburg PA
CBHW031245290426
44109CB00012B/445